MW00510314

INVESTING IN DIVIDEND STOCKS:

A Beginner's Guide to Create a Passive Income and Financial Freedom to Grow Wealth with Powerful Stock Market Strategies. Investing for Retirement Income

MARK SWING

Table of Content

PART ONE:
INTRODUCTION TO DIVIDEND STOCKS

Chapter 1: What Are Dividend Stocks?

Introduction

Companies that are well established tend to spread their earnings among their shareholders. As the company generates profits, it has the chance of spreading them to the individuals that have invested in the company. If you are an investor, these are some of the opportunities that you look forward to, and you find that you are always hoping that you will generate an income from them. In these books, we will discuss details on matters regarding investing in dividend stocks. There is a lot of information that will be acquired by the time you get to the conclusion. Investing in dividend stocks is an investment that could turn your life around. Once you have discovered how it is carried out, and you are aware of the different strategies that you can use, your journey in this industry will be rewarding and amazing. At the same time, it is vital that you understand that the process of acquiring information never stops. As you learn, you need to continually keep learning and at times, unlearn some of the information that you have. With such an approach, you can be assured of success while investing in dividend stocks.

As you decide to invest, one of the main things that you look forward to is the returns you acquire from your investment. You want to ensure that your venture is fruitful and that you do not encounter losses. Even as you come across some risks, you want to be in a position of going past the risk involved. In investments, risk management skills are essential in ensuring that you avoid losses and that you maximize the profits. One of the main characteristics of investors is that they are driven by ambition. You find that they have different goals that they wish to achieve in life. The goals that they have acted as a source of motivation in pushing them towards greater heights. Despite the challenges that they might encounter while investing, they remain hopeful that things will change and that they will live to experience a better day. As an investor, you need to be in a position of accepting the turnout of events. There are times when things are working, and other times things go contrary to what you are expecting. One attribute that you will have to acquire is patience. This is mainly effective during the buy and hold strategies. We shall discuss it better in the book, and you will find out why one will require patience. For beginners that are yet to know much concerning dividend stocks, we shall discuss the importance of investing in dividend stocks and tell you why you should start investing. The book may not have all the information that you need to know, but it points out the critical details that you need to have while getting into the industry.

What Are Dividend Stocks?

A dividend is a distribution of part of the company's earnings from its shareholders. Some companies allow people to invest by purchasing some stocks as they will enable them to be part of the company as shareholders. The boards of directors in a company have the chance of deciding the dividends to be distributed to the shareholders. They also have the opportunity to manage profits. After the board of directors decides on the bonuses, the shareholders have voting rights that they can use to approve the decision made. Dividends are given in the form of shares of as stock, property, or cash dividends. The cash dividends are majorly used as compared to other bonuses. Exchange-traded funds (ETF) and different mutual funds pay dividends. As a company operates, there is a certain amount of profit that it accumulates. This profit is distributed to the shareholders as dividends. The company only shares a portion of its accumulated earnings and gets to retain the remaining. The remaining benefit can be put into different use depending on the preference of the company and the budget they have allocated on the various activities that they carry out.

It is important to note that not all companies follow the same procedure while allocating dividends to the individuals that have invested in the company. You might come across some companies that generate huge profits, bust still, they do not pay their shareholders well. At times, they will earn more benefits that they usually acquire, and yet they fail to increase the dividends that they allocate to their investors. We still have companies that even despite being highly reputed in terms of the profits that they gain, they still fail to pay their dividends on time. As you decide to invest in dividend stocks, these are some of the things that you will have to look at to avoid investing in a company that does not value its clients. The profits may be deceiving and have you thinking that it is a worthy investment, only for you to end up with multiple disappointments. Nowadays, there is plenty of information that we can access online. Some of these vices can be learned from the negative reviews provided by shareholders in a given company. Once you find that other individuals are complaining in a company that you wish to invest in, that should act as a red flag and help you avoid making an investment that you will regret. Still, there are some companies with favorable terms. You find that even when they experience challenges coming up with their usual profits, they always pay their investors the usual amount. This strategy is employed by companies that are maintaining their reputation. They make a decision that is favorable to their shareholders even when they get a loss. Such companies may be challenging to come by, and if you do, it would be wise to invest in the company. It guarantees you value for your money.

The dividends can be paid annually, monthly, or quarterly based on the decision made by the company depending on the board of the directors that govern the company. Apart from the time frame, they get to decide on the dividend rates that they distribute to their shareholders. At times the companies do well and can, therefore, decide to give out special dividends to its shareholders. Different companies experience different levels of growth, which in turn affect their performance. You find that at a given period of time, a company does well and produce a commendable performance. Some companies manage to remain at that stage for long despite the competition that they get. This mainly applies to companies that have managed to build their brand. With such companies, the competition that they encounter does not affect them in any way, and they keep earning their profits. There are moments when the brand does really well and experience a higher benefit than they usually do. In such moments the company may decide to gift its investors by allocating them with special dividends. The publicly listed companies make dividend payments to their investors. The amount payable while the stock is influenced by the dividends allocated by the company. Companies with high dividends have a high stock price, while companies with low dividends have a small stock price. At times you find that the profits earned by a company may not help the investors.

Some companies generate low earnings that you can barely depend on or live by. Not every one that invests in dividend stocks that manage to earn a fortune from it. Some are struggling with peanuts that can hardly support their livelihood. Depending on the company that you decide to invest in, you can either get lucky or unlucky. While deciding on the best company to invest in, you must take this process with a lot of seriousness. Take your time to properly evaluate the options that you have before settling on one. At times you may have little capital to invest, but still, you wish to invest in a venture that will earn you a profit. In such a situation, you can look for a company that has the potential to grow shortly. At the same time, you need to ensure that you do not make a rash decision and end up settling on a company that hardly experiences growth. Some of these predictions are not things that you guess and hope that they will turn out as you expect. You will need to conduct an in-depth survey before concluding. Ensure that you evaluate all the underlying factors while making your prediction. If at all, you have the capital to invest, you can go for the high paying dividends that have the potential of generating a favorable income. Such can guarantee that you earn a fortune from your investment, and this is something that you can be proud of attaining.

Chapter 2: Why Invest in Dividend Stocks

Why Invest in Dividend Stocks?

Generate an Income

One of the main reasons we engage in investments is to earn an income. Some of the beautiful dreams we have to pursue in this world require money. If you desire to travel around the world, you will need a full bank account for you to do so. The most significant percentage of people's lives is spent looking for money that they can get to spend on themselves. For most people, the 9-5 job can barely sustain their livelihood. You find that the majority are working extra hours or having multiple positions to make ends meet. We all have different ambitions in life, which motivate us to do what we want in life. When you have something to live for, it allows you to wake up early and give your best in what you engage in. Ambitions investors are continually looking for what they can do and seeking to engage in new and promising opportunities. If you are such an individual, then investing in dividend stocks can turn out as a gold mine. People have earned a fortune from investing in this venture. Like any other investment, it will demand that an individual becomes strategic while making important decisions.

As you decide to be part of this industry, there are some things that you will be required to learn. If you take your time to properly evaluate the companies that have the potential of giving you high returns, then you can rest assured that you will be raking in the money. In any industry, there will always be one that is making it better than others. The differentiating factor is brought by the different strategies and tactics you both choose to utilize. What I know is that, if you are a wise investor, the probability of minting millions from this venture is high. Dividend stocks have been a real game-changer to many. For anyone hoping to invest in dividend stocks, this is a decision that you will not regret. It is a perfect venture for anyone looking forward to boosting their income. You might also be in a phase where you would like to try out something different and new. All you will have to do is gain a proper understanding of how it works, and you will be ready to soar high. Some have managed to get to levels whereby it's their primary source of income. Anyone can get to this point as long as they master the art of investing in dividend stocks.

Earn Profits and Acquire Ownership

Once you buy your stock from a given company, you receive ownership. For some, knowing that they own shares in a given company, is something that they are proud of. Well recognized companies that have managed to build a brilliant brand that looks promising tend to have many investors getting on board. However, we have had cases whereby some well-known brands have fallen due to issues like mismanagement of funds or poor management. Such situations may, at times, be unpredictable, and once they occur, there is nothing much that we can do apart from accepting the turnout of events. One can, however, predict some of these events by carrying out an excellent analysis of the companies records. If you encounter some red flags that should automatically make you avoid that particular company. Having a mentor can also ease this process for you. They can offer some guidance on the best companies to deal with for the sake of generating profits from dividend stocks. The fantastic thing about being alive in this century is that the internet has been brought to make work easier for us. You find that there is a lot of information available on websites, blogs, social media, and other platforms. Once you decide to invest in dividend stocks, you can quickly check out what different companies have to offer. At the same time, you want to invest in a company that has the potential for growth in terms of the revenue generated.

Investing in dividends is a perfect way to multiply your savings. You find that we work hard and store money in a savings account. Some generate profits, while others do not. Instead of having a traditional way of saving, how about investing in that money. While you invest, you can double those savings to an incredible amount that you will be happy about. The beauty of investing is that you get more added to the little that you had. As we keep advancing in the 21st century, money is becoming a top priority. Almost everything that one needs to do requires payment. For instance, the thought of traveling around the world is impressive and ideally nearly every person's dream. However, to get to that point, one has to have secured the bag. With some few but productive investments, this is possible. Instead of storing the money where it does not grow, go out of your way, and invest in dividend stocks. I am positive that this is a move that you will not regret. If you are one that fears to engage in things because they seem technical or complicated, you have nothing to fear in dividend stocks. For a person who is ready and willing to learn, this is an investment idea that you can quickly grasp and come around. Instead of getting comfortable tapping the ocean, get in the waters, and learn to swim. After all, they say you can never know until you try; dividend stocks are an ideal investment.

Capital Appreciation

Every investor aspires to invest in something that adds value. When I buy something from a store at $10 for selling, I hope that as I sell to my clients, I will earn an extra penny from what I spent. Numerous factors can influence the percentage of profit. You'll find one selling at $15 and another at $20. The price narrows down to the value that we give each product. I believe that the cost is not always reliant on the quality, but rather it can be diverse. A seller could have value for their product and decide to overprice it.

On the other hand, a buyer can have value for a given product and decide to purchase it at any given price. Regardless of how we view value, certain products increase in value over a given duration. Different factors can influence the increase in value. Companies have the potential of increasing in value. At the start of any given company, the founders have big dreams of it becoming a big company. New ventures are like babies, and one has to be keen while nurturing them to ensure that they become productive and amazing people. Well, the same applies to companies. In the beginning, each action and step took matters, and any wrong move can send you home faster than you could have imagined.

Some companies turn out being successful while others fail before they get on their feet. One of the critical factors in a company is the product or service that they offer and the management. In terms of product, the company needs to ensure that their product is better than that of its competitors. If at all the products are the same, there needs to be a unique feature that sets it apart from others. In terms of management, functional management guarantees a thriving institution. We have had many institutions close due to poor management. While deciding on the best dividend stocks to invest in, these are some of the factors that you ought to consider. One of the best things about some institutions is that they manage to grow over the years and therefore increase their revenue. With the right management and product, a company can guarantee capital appreciation. When you manage to invest in a company that generates profits each year, your investment in dividend stocks is guaranteed capital appreciation. One crucial step that you keenly need to analyze before engaging in dividend stocks is the company that you wish to invest in. Making a wise choice will guarantee you a secured constant income from your investment.

As you spend, one of your top goals is to ensure that your gains go above your initial investment. You find that a company with the right management and one that has established its product is likely to undergo capital appreciation. Ideally, it is the dream of every investor to invest in such a company.

Rely on Buy and Hold Advantage

In the purchase and hold advantage, one secures stocks and keeps them on hold for a while until they increase in value. After that, they can sell them at a more significant profit. Currently, most entrepreneurs are employing such strategies. The food industry is the most affected in those terms. You find that most foodstuffs are seasonal. When any fruit, legume, or vegetable is in season, its production tends to be high. The production level may, at times exceed the demand. This causes a reduction in prices. At that point, the majority of the individuals or companies selling that product may end up incurring losses or meager profits. This destabilizes growth and hence interferes with some activities. To avoid some of these instances, the sellers can keep the product until it is out of season, or its production level increases. When its availability in the market reduces, they can reintroduce it to the buyers. At this point, they can sell at their required price, or they can slightly increase the costs to earn more profit. This strategy is usually more beneficial to the producer as opposed to the consumer. Some sellers may misuse this to double their earnings, and hence it is unfavorable to the consumer. To exercise this, one needs to have some patience for them to be willing to wait until the prices are favorable for them to engage in a given market.

How does this strategy help an individual investing in dividend stocks? Well, companies experience different phases as they grow. There are times when the business is doing well, and at the same time, they may experience some challenges in the industry. There are different factors influencing the productivity of institutions. There are moments when they are experiencing an increase in profits, and at the same time, there are moments when they incur losses. During the period when the company is not doing well, some people tend to sell their shares at a throwaway price. At that point, one may think that the future is not promising and hence withdraw their shares. Some investors decide to evaluate the condition further so that they can know if there is a potential of the company doing well in the future. Once they have carried out their analysis, they can decide to stay and wait until the value of the stocks increases.

On the other hand, the company may not be experiencing losses but is encountering constant growth. Judging from the revenue that a company has been generating over the years, you may discover that it is continuously battling consistent growth. For instance, if a share went for $6 in 2010, it might be $20 in 2018.

During that period, you may decide not to do anything with your shares until their value doubles. At this point, you can earn more than you had anticipated from your stocks. In this case, the buy and hold strategy will be helpful.

Chapter 3: How to Get Started with Stocks

How to Get Started with Stocks

Whenever you anticipate joining any industry, one of the things that you look forward to learning is how it operates. Well, if you are a newbie in the stock industry, below are some points that you will have to consider before getting started. The points discussed are generally what you can consider while engaging in any stock and not specific to dividend stocks.

Conduct Research on Stocks

Carrying out research is the most crucial factor that an individual needs to consider. One cannot engage in an activity that they do not understand unless they are setting themselves up for failure. We have had situations whereby people engage in activities before fully understanding what they entail. After they encounter a setback, they make conclusions that the investments they made were not worth their while. With the right information, you can avoid some of these incidences from occurring. There are many places where you can acquire this information. You can read books, get content online, or get information from attending some training sessions. It is also important to note that learning never ends. As the stock industry expands and diversifies, there are new things that are coming up. When this occurs, you have to keep up with the latest information being provided.

Currently, there are different stocks that one can invest in. Each operates differently, and they have their pros and cons. In this book, we are discussing on dividend stocks. You can get information regarding the other types of capital from different resources. Before engaging in any stock, one has to do thorough research on the stock. This makes one more conversant with it and places them at a position of making wise investments. At times we attend some training sessions and get all hyped regarding investing in the stocks. The anticipations that we have to make us make quick decisions that we may end up regretting. To avoid getting in such, ensure that you get the proper information regarding the stock that you wish to invest in. We at times complicate things, yet they are easy and straight forward. In this context, we make the learning process appear like something that demands much of your time. To make this process easier, you can commit an hour in your day to learning. For instance, you could decide that the first hour after you wake up is deliberately spent to gain knowledge on stocks. Once you make this a continuous process, it gets more comfortable for you to adopt it as part of your daily routine quickly. You can plan it depending on how busy your schedule is, and with time you will be well equipped and ready to invest in the preferred stock.

Set Goals

When we set goals, great things happen. We come across this statement a lot, but how often do we take it with the seriousness that it requires? You will attend a training session, and one of the questions that the speaker may ask is, do you have goals for your life? Amazing things happen when we set goals and work hard towards accomplishing them. The goals that we set can act as a motivating tool. Take, for instance, a team that has qualified for the finals. The primary purpose of the team at that instance is to emerge as the winner. In such an example, they give their best in what they do to get what they want. While swing trading, you need to come up with some goals. Such goals help you try harder and give your best in the various activities that you undertake. You may encounter some challenges, but the goals you have will act as a reminder as to why you engaged in the trade in the first place. While setting the goals, make sure that they are realistic. For instance, you cannot be making an investment of 600USD and expect to earn a million. Set an anticipated profit that is slightly higher than your investment. This will prevent you from getting disappointed.

After setting the goals, make it a habit to remind yourself about the goals that you have set regularly. You can make it part of your morning routine whereby you go through your investment goals as you ensure that you give your best towards achieving them. As you start your journey in investing in stocks, ensure that you set some goals that you work hard towards achieving. For instance, you might decide that in the next seven years, you look forward to getting into the real estate business from finances acquired from investing in stocks. As an individual that has decided to engage in dividend stocks, this can act as a significant driving force towards scaling to a greater height. It allows you to have something to live for. At times the road might get bumpy, and you feel like giving up or losing hope; however, the goals that you have to keep you focused and allow you to push beyond your limits. We, at times, set low expectations for ourselves and wonder why we are not making progress as required. It's about time we break free from a limitation mentality, and we expand our boundaries. Anytime you invest in the dividend stocks, and you keep reminding yourself of the goal that you have in mind. In this case, the real estate business is the big picture. It allows you to retain focus and give the best results in what you do. As you look into the stocks that you wish to invest, also consider setting goals that make your investment worth your while and ensure that you are entirely rooted in it.

Identify the Amount of Money You Are Willing to Invest

One of the most asked questions by beginners is the amount of money that they need to use while investing in stocks. In the beginning, one feels like they do not know much about a venture, so they want to start with a small investment. It is okay to feel like that, and you have the right to feel that way. While investing in stocks, you can begin with a small investment. This factor is very convenient, especially if you are a beginner. You can engage in an investment that requires high capital, yet you have little knowledge of how it is carried out. Instead of making a profit, you end up spending a lot of capital and encountering losses. You have to know how to manage your finances for you to last long the investment venture. The amount of money you spend while investing can, at times, be determined by your performance in previous investments. If you notice that your last investments are performing well, you can keep spending. However, if you realize that you are making more losses than profits that should act as an indicator that you need to take a break.

The most significant mistake the majority of investors are making is that they keep engaging in trades even when they encounter losses. You keep losing money, and the trades that you make do not benefit you in any way. Once the damages are more, that should act as a sign for you to stop investing in that stock. During that period, you can evaluate the progress you have made and see what you are doing wrong. At the same time, you can identify the things that you are doing right. After carrying out that analysis, you can quickly know the right way forward. Another dangerous move that some people make is trying to cover up for losses incurred from previous investments by making other investments. Without making a proper evaluation, you cannot decide on the next step to make. Most decisions made when our mind is not clear, end up frustrating us, and as a result, we incur the losses. To avoid such incidences from affecting you, ensure that you carry out excellent research before reinvesting. This evaluation allows you to identify where you went wrong, and you can also come up with the best strategies that can help you in the next trade. By doing this, you manage to save money since you only get to invest when you are guaranteed to earn huge returns. The decisions that we make while investing in stocks play a significant role in determining the fate of our investment. Any wrong decision made can make one lose money faster than expected. It is also advisable that one does not place all their eggs in one basket. In case anything comes up, you need to be in a position that you do not acquire complete loss. Your finances are essential, and when making decisions regarding them, one needs to make the right choices.

Decide on the Stock That You Wish to Invest In

Knowing the best stocks is beneficial as it influences the profits you will earn at the end of the day. You have the potential to make high returns or make losses. This possibility is controlled by a number of decisions that you make while investing. Identifying the best stock to engage in happens to be one of the decisions that you need to make. While carrying out this process, try to avoid recently introduced stocks. Lack of experience can pose a challenge to the company. Try looking for the stocks that have had a longer time in the market. Such can guarantee the potential of earning returns. In the process of searching for the best stocks to trade, take some time to analyze the stock market to see the performance of the different commodities. Invest in those that show consistency in their production; such trades have a high likelihood of earning your profits. Remember to take your time and not to rush in making conclusions. Selecting the most suitable stocks is a crucial process for any investor. High chances are, it will determine how your investment turns out. The method of choosing the best stock is very vital for anyone looking into investing. There are different stocks that an individual can engage in. There are some pros and cons to participating in the various types of stocks.

While selecting the best stock to ensure that you conduct a proper background check on the stock you wish to engage in. While carrying out this process, you will identify that the best stock has higher reviews and ratings as compared to the other commodities. Get to know what people have to say regarding individual stocks. Negative feedbacks should act as a warning to ensure that you do not engage in the given stocks. On the other hand, positive feedbacks will encourage you to start trading in some commodities. Having the right information will help you a lot in this process and make things easier. The stock you choose will determine how your investment will be. If you aim at earning huge profits, you need to select the best stocks. If you decide to invest in dividend stocks, there are some factors that you will have to consider. For instance, one of the crucial processes will involve selecting the company that you intend to invest in. It is essential since it will have a high impact on the returns that your investment will give you. If you want to earn high profits, you will require a well-established company that has a reputation for offering good dividends. This selection ensures that you gain from the dividend stocks. As you select the best stocks to invest in, it is essential that you avoid making hast decisions and conclusions. Take your time to study each share as you come up with reasons why you should invest in them and at the same time, come up with reasons why you should avoid investing in them.

Get a Mentor

Currently, people appreciate the need for a mentor in their life. Life can get overwhelming to the point of requiring help to go about the various phases of life. One of the fantastic things about a coach or mentor is that they can guide you in the right path and direction to follow. They are able to create footprints, and all that is left for us to do is follow. We can evaluate the effect of a coach in a soccer match. Anytime the team is about to play any game, the work of the coach is to prepare them. He knows each player in the group and has the chance to select some. The coach takes some time to study each player and knows their weaknesses and strengths. It is his obligation to place the players at positions they can best perform based on what they are good at. You find that he comes up with some strategies that will give his players an upper hand while playing. The game never changes, and neither does its rules, but it is how the teams play that changes the game. The teams with the best strategy and plan will succeed over the other side.

How is a mentor effective to an investor? The investment industry is a sensitive industry, and without guidance, you may experience some challenges before you make it to your desired point. We can equate investing in playing a game. In this case, your success is influence y how well you play and the strategies that you utilize to ensure that you remain at the top. A mentor has been in the field longer than you have, and this allows them to gain the relevant experience in the given area. The information that they have places them at a position of offering sound advice that can guide you in achieving the best. You find that the stocks never change, but it is the strategy that improves. Get an individual who has more experience in investing in the capital that you wish to invest in and one that can help you while investing. Such people can help you come up with a proper investment plan and give you some of the success tips that you can utilize to become a better investor. While choosing one ensure that you run a quick background check just to ensure that it is an individual that can help you. The process of finding a good mentor has been made easier with the help of the internet. You can quickly get reviews concerning a particular individual from people that have already had business with them. Such studies are useful while making the right decisions, and as a result, you end up with a good mentor that can help you while investing in stocks. One should avoid making rash decisions while getting a suitable mentor. It is also good to get an individual that you easily connect with.

Attend Various Training Sessions

At times the different companies dealing with individual stocks have some training sessions. Such pieces of training are more of a market strategy for them since, after training, you may like what they do and decide to invest with them. Such an approach is right because they make you aware of who they are and what you are engaging in before committing to it. On the other hand, it makes it easier for you to make a decision on the best stock to invest in. In some of these training, one can learn a lot. At times you may not have the time to learn everything on your own. It becomes better if you find an individual that can simplify the information that you need in a single training session. As you start your journey in investing ensure that you do not miss out on some of these sessions. We also have some clubs that decide to invest in ventures that can earn returns. As a club, you can come together and organize a training session. In such events, one has to pay some fee to the individual conducting the meeting. The good thing is that you will be parting with some amount of your money and in the process, learn how to make more money.

You can also decide to come together as a group of friends willing to learn more about stocks and look for an excellent trainer. While selecting a good trainer, ensure that you get an experienced person who will teach you well and make it easy for you to start trading. There are different stocks that you can choose to invest in. As a group, you can decide to narrow down to three or two stocks and get experienced individuals to speak on them. After you acquire information from the different sources, come up with a table that indicates the pros and cons of engaging in each stock. From the knowledge that you have acquired, you can choose the capital that you find more favorable to invest in. This process does not require much from the individuals concerned. All you will have to do is part with a few coins as you learn and spend some of your time in training. Instead of investing blindly, this is an excellent strategy to utilize. It ensures that you make the right decision while investing in stocks. In the training sessions, you can also identify other stocks that you were not aware of. You may find that some of them have the potential of providing returns once you invest in them. This knowledge gives you the chance to know new opportunities that you can use. For instance, you might not be aware of dividend stocks, and in one of the training sessions, you learn about it and find it to be a good investment. Having acquired this information, you can decide to invest in dividend stocks. Generally, these training sessions are useful in helping us make the right investment decisions.

Investing in Dividend Stocks

Select the Best Company to Invest In

Different companies offer different dividend stocks. Selecting the best company to invest in is a crucial process that will demand your time and concentration while making the right decision. You cannot randomly choose any company. There is research that you will need to carry out on the different companies as you look for favorable factors that encourage one to invest in them. As an investor, you will be looking for companies that protect your investment and those that guarantee huge returns from the investments that you make. In most cases, you find that the companies that have already established themselves have a high likelihood of attracting investors as compared to the recently established companies. Once they are well established, they manage to create a long-lasting brand that everyone trusts. As a result, they experience a consistent flow of capital, and hence they are in a position of healthily providing dividends to their investors. This allows them to remain relevant in the industry that they are in, and despite the existence of competition, they manage to keep succeeding and generating revenue. Such companies are the best to invest in and ensure that you have a regular flow of finances. At times the company may decide to increase its dividends as the capital gain increases. You find that investors benefit from such moves, and that is how some have managed to earn a fortune from investing in dividend stocks.

Acquire the Needed Knowledge on Dividend Stocks

Anytime you decide to do something you have never done before, the first measure you will take is learning more about it. This applies to dividend stocks; you cannot become a successful investor unless you know what it entails. As an investor, there are plenty of ventures to engage in. We are now in a space where people are appreciating investing in intangible products as long as they earn from it. You will come across stories of many people who have engaged in dividend stocks and made a fortune out of it. Having acquired this information, you decide to participate in the venture and start investing without receiving the needed information. In the process, you end up making a loss, and you regret why you engaged in the first place. To avoid such frustrations, ensure that you acquire all the knowledge that you need to succeed in the industry. It is also essential to note that learning is not only applicable as you begin; you need to learn even when you become an expert.

One of the best ways to keep winning and stay on top is consistency. Make each day a learning day. As this industry grows, you will realize that new things are coming up. What worked the previous day, may not work in the present. Knowing this keeps us grounded and helps us improve on what we know. Some of these tricks will ensure that you become an expert while investing. Your ability to gain knowledge and use it well can give you an added advantage as opposed to an individual with more years of experience. Their experience may not matter if they lack knowledge. As a beginner, you can decide to gain all the understanding that you need and become better than individuals who started earlier. The investment strategies also play an essential role in guaranteeing your success. Ensure that you are well aware of all the strategies that you can utilize. It is also recommended that you have a plan that directs you on what to do.

Track Your Performance

Once in a while, it's good to find out how you are performing.

The main aim of engaging in investments is to make progress through the earnings that you make. In the beginning, you may encounter specific challenges; hence, your profits may not be high. However, as you progress, there are a lot of things that you learn along the way. Such lessons make it possible to trade and earn. Beginnings may be rough, but with the right attitude, you can transform your journey into investing in dividend stocks. The game-changer in this field is merely learning and never getting tired of the learning process. One of the best things about tracking one's performance is that you determine if you are making progress or if it's an all massacre affair. Knowing this helps in decision making. You get to change your way of doing things based on the discoveries that you make. For instance, if you note that you are barely earning from the dividends that you invest in, that should act as a red flag. It allows you to identify the cause of the problem and can discover ways through which you can make an improvement. You can also determine the seasons you made successful sales and come up with some investment strategies.

Have a place whereby you indicate the various activities that you carry out while investing in dividend stocks. Writing down the investments that you make helps you in tracking the progress that you are making and helps you in improving in areas that need improvement. The journal can also act as a reference point. You can quickly identify the stocks that earned you a profit. The knowledge acquired can be used in making the right trade decisions. On the other hand, you get to know the types of investments that you should avoid, especially when you do not want to make a loss. You can also indicate the plans that you have in your journal. It acts as a reminder and helps you in pursuing them. Having some of your goals written down can act as a source of motivation towards achieving them. Every day that you wake up, you get to review them and work hard towards achieving them. There is also some power in tracking your progress just to see how far you are going and get to know the various challenges that you are facing while investing. This knowledge provides room for improvement and makes you do better. As an investor, one of the qualities that you will be required to exercise is patience. You will continuously need to keep reminding yourself why you chose to invest in the first place. It is not every day that you will happily walk to the bank smiling. At times you will be expected to trust the process hoping that things will turn out as you expect them to. However, when you can track your progress, you can easily make the right investment decisions.

Chapter 4: Key Technical Terms

Key Technical Terms

Dividends

A reward is given by a company as a token of appreciation to the shareholders for investing in the company's equity. The bonus is obtained from the company's profits. Different companies will offer various dividends depending on their ability and policies made by the board of directors.

Retained Earnings

The net income remaining in the company after it has paid its shareholders their dividends. Companies do not distribute all their profits to their investors; instead, they get to retain some. The remaining benefits can be utilized in different ways by the companies in ensuring that they remain in business.

Special Dividends

This is a one-time distribution of payments to the shareholders. This is done in the form of cash. The amount of money paid in special dividends is higher than the dividend amounts that are usually paid. Exclusive bonuses mainly occur when a company earns more than its anticipated profits. Such dividends are ordinary in well-established companies that have managed to build a strong brand. There are periods where they receive more amount of money than they anticipated, and this allows them to keep growing. When a company's profits as moving well, it makes it possible to create a better and more defined brand that can be trusted by many. They also get to increase the quality of the products or services that they offer. This factor gives them a better advantage over their competitors. With such influencing factors, it is possible to come up with special dividends.

Board of Directors

The board of directors represents the shareholders in a company, and they are usually elected. Their work is to hold meetings aimed at overseeing the company's performance and setting policies that aid in management. For all public companies, it is a requirement that they have a board of directors being tasked with oversight on the performance of the company. We also have some private companies that have a board of directors. The main job that the individuals do is ensuring that they act as a link between the company and the other investors. They may not necessarily represent the investors, but they can serve the consumers using the products or services provided by the company. In terms of investing in dividend stocks, it is the board of directors that ensure they make the right choices on behalf of the other shareholders. Part of the roles that they play includes; coming up with options policies, coming up with dividend policies, executive compensation, and the hiring and firing of senior executives. We cannot underestimate the role played by the board of directors as they are tasked with critical roles in the organization. The decisions that they make have an impact on the output of a company. For instance, the hiring and firing of senior executives is an essential task to be assigned. These individuals determine the direction in which the company will move through their leadership. A company with good leadership has the potential of going far.

Fiduciary

This is an organization or person that acts as a representative for other people in managing assets. They need to be well trusted by the individuals that they are representing for them to perform their duties effectively. The fiduciary may be tasked with managing assets and finances at times, ensuring the wellbeing of the individual that has entrusted them as their representative. The law might require that they are ethnically bound so that they carry out the various activities in the person's best interest. Some examples of individuals with fiduciary duties include; board of directors, cooperative officers, accountants, financial advisors, executors, and bankers, among others. Once an individual accepts fiduciary responsibilities, they fully accept to act on behalf of the other individual. Any decision that they make directly impacts the individuals that have entrusted them with the task. Once you take up fiduciary duties, you need to ensure that you act accordingly.

Inside Director

This is someone that is employed by the company and is part of the board of directors. They can also be a direct stakeholder or officer. Like other board members, the inside director has fiduciary duties representing the company. Their work is to link the outside directors with what happens in the company and ensure that they serve them well by providing the views and position that the company holds to its shareholders. They also need adequate knowledge of the working of the company for them to ensure that they give the best feedback to the outside directors. The inside directors play a significant role in a company as they provide that they guarantee the success of the company. The inside directors are mainly executives in a company. They are known by terms such as chief executive officers (CEO), chief operating officers (COO), and chief financial officers (CFO). For them to effectively guarantee the success of a company, the inside directors have to be people with the right qualifications. We have companies that collapse due to poor management. This is perhaps the worst reason for the failure of a given venture.

Institutional Investor

This can be an organization or an individual that trades

securities to acquire lower commissions and preferential treatment. They can purchase large shares all at once, and you may find that they are the most prominent stakeholders. An institutional investment usually invests in the place of its members. The challenge with this investment is that they are not well protected. It is assumed that they fully understand how the investment works, and hence, they hardly get any protection. You are mainly aware of this investment type through insurance companies. It can be part of an insurance package, depending on the insurance company that you deal with. There are different types of institution managers. They include; insurance companies, pension funds, mutual funds hedge funds, and commercial banks. In case you are afraid of investing on your own, you can invest through institutional investors. It's a more secure investment, especially for an individual that is unable to spend on their own.

Voting Rights

The shareholders have the chance on issues concerning corporate policy and making decisions on the selection of the board of directors. With voting rights, individuals can make a difference in the corporate sector by voting towards change. In the corporate area, there are a lot of factors affecting the operation of a company. Some of these factors may be overlooked and cause the collapse of businesses that were promising. We can avoid such incidences from occurring through the board of directors. These individuals ensure that the parties involved play their role effectively so that the company's operations may continue as planned. It is effortless for the management or leadership in an institution to cause the collapse of a company. When the administration is not right, there might be cases of mismanagement of funds. In some cases, with the wrong leadership, the workers become demotivated. You find that their productivity is not maximized and hence resulting in low performances. This factor, in turn, affects the overall output of the company, and they fail to produce good results. Some of these factors can be observed by the board of directors. Once they discover that something is not working as it should, they can vote against it. For instance, if there is a problem with the management, they can decide to do away with it by casting votes. Even as they select the new management, they can cast votes. At times they may want to implement some company policies, which require voting rights. This allows them to go with the decision that has been agreed upon by the majority of the members.

Profits

This may not be a technical term since the majority knows what it entails. A profit is a capital gain that we acquire after subtracting the buying price from the selling price. For companies, the production cost acts as the buying price. It is the dream of all companies to get profits. The income we generate from the different services and products that we offer, determine if we stay in business or not. Individuals, as well as institutions, are continually looking for new ways to minimize the losses as they maximize their profits. As we invest in dividends, a percentage of the amount that we get comes from the profits that the company has accumulated. Some companies generate more returns than others, and hence, they manage to give higher dividends to their shareholders. As you invest, one of the things you aim to do, it getting a company that pays well, and therefore it can guarantee that you will continuously get an income. While selecting the best company to invest in, there are a number of factors that you will seriously have to take into consideration. For instance, you could check at the history of the company to find out how they allocate their dividends and their consistency in doing that. As you keep reading, you will come across an in-depth explanation of the factors to consider.

Chapter 5: Technical and Fundamental Analysis

Technical and Fundamental Analysis

Technical Analysis

Technical analysis involves predicting the expected future price of an asset or a financial instrument using volume data and historical price. The technical analysis mainly focuses on the price. All the conclusions that are made are drawn from the analysis made are based on the price. We have different types of technical analysis, and they include; candlestick charting, Dow Theory, and Elliott wave theory. These theories utilize price trends and price patterns to predict future prices. As you invest in dividend stocks, one of the main factors that you will consider is the rates given to different dividend stocks. Ideally, you will look forward to investing in a stock that appreciates in value. Companies that have an increase in the dividend stocks as the profits increase are the best to invest in, especially if you are looking forward to earning a fortune from your investment. The price movements can help you determine if it is a worthy investment to make or if you should avoid engaging in it at all costs. You can use the different methods of technical analysis while looking at the price movements. From the information that you get, you can decide if you will invest in that dividend stock or not. This method can be useful in helping one make the right decisions. In investments, the prices play a significant role, and when you can determine the price moment, you can easily make wise investment decisions.

Fundamental Analysis

Fundamental analysis involves analyzing the financial statement through examining the management, products, and services, market, economic environment, and the economic environment. In this analysis, some of the data used include; assets, revenue, dividends, liabilities, profits, and expenses. It also involves critical ratios such as dividend payout ratio, the price per earnings ratio, returns on equity, and dividend yields. This analysis aids in providing detail information concerning a given company. One can compare the data and the ratios involved while coming up with an analysis. This information is essential to an investor since they get to know the best stocks to invest in. You might be tied between investing in two different stocks. However, after this analysis, one can quickly identify the most suitable stock. There are many factors influencing the earnings derived from a given investment. Unlike technical analysis, the fundamental analysis considers all the possible factors that can influence the performance of a stock. It is important for an individual that requires detailed information. As you intend to invest in dividend stocks, you get all the information that guides you in making good investment choices. Having looked at the various factors influencing that performance of a company, one can easily determine if the company has a consistent flow of income. A company that is performing well in what it does can easily assure one that it will be a worthwhile investment. This analysis is essential for all the individuals' looking forward to investing in dividend stocks.

PART TWO:
HOW IT WORKS

Chapter 6: Investing in Dividend Stock Strategies

Investing in Dividend Stock Strategies

In any investment, you find that there are certain strategies that one needs to utilize. A strategy makes the investment worthwhile and at times, guarantees the success of the given investment. There are many challenges that we encounter while investing in different stocks. We have to come up with ways in which we can overcome some of these challenges and perform better at what we do. As you learn more about dividend stocks, you get to know more about the challenges that you will likely encounter. At the same time, you can easily come up with strategies that you can utilize to succeed in the industry. There is power in having unique strategies that you can use to carry different activities. They allow you to achieve more than you could have anticipated and make the process easier for you. At times having the right strategies can protect you from incurring losses. We invest with the aim of earning profits. You find that we try all that we can to minimize the potential risks that may sabotage our investment. Losses are the last thing you want to encounter as an investor; it is incredible that with the right strategy, you can easily manage to do this.

We can use examples of companies that have grown due to the fact that they had the right strategy. In a competitive business sector, the different companies are always trying to remain relevant in the industry. You find that they have to come up with ways in which they provide a better output than their consumers. At times the product is the same across the board, but how it is delivered to its consumers makes the difference. In this instance, the producer has to come up with different strategies that allow the product to sell to the consumers. There are certain factors that the company will consider. One of the elements will involve studying the behavior of the consumer. What the consumer wants is something that the producer has to deliver without compromise, for them to remain loyal to the brand. To achieve this, there are specific mechanisms and policies that the company will put in place. The strategies that they utilize have to get them the clients that they want and at the same time, generate an income for them. Those with the best plans manage to stay on top and have a successful business. Below are some of the strategies that one can utilize.

Invest in Companies That Have High Dividends

As a wise investor, one would invest in a well-performing company. For instance if I had a company A that generates a revenue of $10 billion annually and another company B that generates $100 million annually, one would go for company A. you find that company A has already established its name, and therefore it encounters consistent capital gain, which guarantees that you earn your dividends as an investor. At the same time, you discover that it has managed to get clients that are intoxicated in the brand. This factor makes them keep purchasing the products or services from that particular company. Even when competition arises, the consumers are still satisfied with the brand and keep purchasing from it. For a company to get to this point, they also need to be strategic at how they handle the different clients. They have to be careful to ensure that at the beginning, they carefully evaluate the market they are targeting and find out what the consumers want. At the initial stages, there are a lot of compromises to be made; at this point, the companies first want to understand their market. Once this is done, they know what to deliver, and they take advantage of that to get clients on board. After all is done, and they acquire many users that are intoxicated in the brand, you find that no matter the amount of money they charge for different services and products, the consumers still support.

As an investor, you should target such companies. They guarantee a constant flow of dividends, and hence, as you invest, you are sure that it will bring back returns. At times you may not necessarily rely on already established companies. You might come across some companies that have not been in operation for long, but they are experiencing growth annually. You will be surprised by how fast the company can move from one level to another. These entire factors are influenced by different conditions surrounding the company. When the conditions are favorable, then the company is likely to experience tremendous growth. On the other hand, when the conditions are not favorable, the company may not experience growth. You can decide to invest in the company that shows potential for growth as you wait for the dividends to increase. However, it is important to note that some companies experience growth over a very short duration of time, and it may not last for long. When you invest in such, you may end up making losses. To avoid this, ensure that you properly evaluate the situation at hand before making a hasty decision to invest in the company. While analyzing, there are certain discoveries that you might make, that act as red flags for you to invest in the company.

Dividends That Are Consistent

You want to ensure that you have a constant flow of income. This can be made possible by investing in a company that is highly reputed for paying its dividends to the investors without fail. Getting such a company demands that you do your research well, for you to land on the best. While doing this, there are some factors that you can look at. For instance, you can evaluate the consistency or frequency of a company in terms of paying dividends to the investors. You will be surprised that despite the high income generated by some well-established companies, they still fail to pay dividends on time. Being consistent in what you do is important since it guarantees competence. This aspect can be applied in various aspects of life apart from companies offering dividends. For instance, we can study the success rates of students in a school. You find that there are those that are consistent in maintaining the top position. In case there is a competition coming up, or if anything needs to be done that involves academics, they will be considered first. That conclusion is met due to their consistency in what they do and as a result, the earn eligibility for certain positions. This factor is also considered while investing in dividend stocks. You find that you want to invest in an investment that is steady and healthy.

It is unfortunate that some companies give inaccurate information on the revenue that they generate. This behavior is very common in newly established companies since all they aspire to do is to attract the investors. They do so with the intention of acquiring more capital to develop the business. Such a strategy is very wrong as it harms the investor in cases where the anticipated figures are altered. The investors to earn a lot at the end, only for them to end up with huge frustrations and regrets as to why they engaged in the investment. To avoid loss from such, you can avoid investing in such companies. Alternatively, you can carry out further research on how real the figures are. With proper research, you can find some loopholes that indicate you should avoid the given investment. Many investors have ended up in this trap. A company offers an attractive offer that seems too good to be true. You begin to dream of how your dividends will increase over the years, and you end up making your investment. Before you know it, you end up making a loss as the company falls or remains stagnant. In such incidence, you may discover that the company does not incur a huge loss. They manage to do this y pulling resources from different sources. By doing so, the losses incurred, do not greatly affect them. When you decide to invest in dividend stocks, this is one of the key factors that you will have to consider. Carrying out a proper evaluation on the item you intend to invest in, will inhibit you from making some of these mistakes.

Dividends That Have the Potential to Grow

Growth is a process that we aspire to achieve in different aspects of our lives. It is incredibly amazing how different creatures experience growth. We can use the example of a human being. It starts from a fetus in the womb, and after birth, we have a child. The child encounters different stages of growth from a toddler, puberty, young adult, adult, and finally, the elderly. All these stages occur at their given time and are experienced differently. At the different stages, there are some factors influencing the growth process, and they determine how effective that stage will be for the individual involved. The same applies to dividend stocks. There are some companies that are making it more than others. You find that a company may start off with a small dividend at the beginning and experiences some growth that allows the company to offer higher dividends. There are certain factors affecting the growth of a company. These factors allow the company to develop, and at times we can predict the potential growth based on the direction that the company is moving. As you are carrying out your research regarding a given company, these are points that you can pick up. One can easily identify a company that has the potential to grow, and you can seize the opportunity to invest in such. Such a strategy can help you earn a fortune from investing in dividend stocks.

On the other hand, there are some companies that offer a one-time profit and suddenly collapse or experience slow development. As I mentioned earlier, most such companies tend to new, and therefore, they utilize that strategy to attract investors. You are pleased with the revenue that the company generates at the beginning, and that attracts you to invest in the company. Before you know it, the company collapses, and you end up losing your investment. One ought to be careful to avoid being a victim of such traps. Ensure that you do your research well since it is something that you can easily identify as long as you conduct your evaluation well. As a wise investor, the best place to invest would be a company that is experiencing growth. You are assured that you will earn more dividends in the future, and therefore, it is a perfect way to secure your investment.

All the above factors act as good strategies or factors we need to consider before investing in dividend stocks. There are people making it from investing in dividend stocks, and as a beginner, you might aspire to get in the position that they are in. With the right strategies, this can be made possible. You, too can start earning a fortune like others that are already making it in the industry. Some of these strategies can be created once we dedicate our time and energy in doing proper research on the dividend stocks. There is a lot to be learned, and we can never fully exhaust everything.

Chapter 7: The Best Time to Buy Dividend Stocks

The Best Time to Buy Dividend Stocks

Is there a really perfect time to buy dividend stocks? This is a question asked by most investors before investing in dividend stocks. Well, for us to identify the best time to purchase dividend stocks, one of the key considerations one has to make is the company one wishes to invest in. When looking at the company, there are certain characteristics or qualities that the investment needs to uphold for it to be a trustworthy institution to conduct business with. In matters of investing, one needs to be careful while making decisions regarding the investment that they which to engage in. One cannot commit their money in something that does not have the potential to yield profits. So, to avoid such incidences from occurring, it is important that you take your time to evaluate the stakes involved before engaging in the investment. We will discuss come qualities that you need to look at in investment and which will help you know the best time to purchase dividend stocks.

The History of the Company

The history allows us to know more about the potential of the company and how far it can go in the future. Companies that have been in operation for more years are better preferred than the newly established companies. When a company has been recently established, it's slightly difficult to predict where it will be in the years to come. There are certain factors that will influence its productivity. For instance, they may have a good product that they are unable to push to the market. As it is being established, it requires a good marketing strategy for it to push into the already existing market. The company needs to find ways in which it can create a lasting brand for itself. Failure to employ some of these strategies will cause the company to fall long before it rises to its feet. We have had instances where newly established companies are seeking investors to invest in the industry long before they rose to their feet. They give promises of giving back dividends over a short duration since they believe that their product will sell. However, things go wrong, and they are unable to deliver what they promised. Many investors have lost money from such companies. Before one invests in such, it is advisable that you look at how realistic the plan of the company is for you to know if it is a worthwhile investment.

For already established companies, there is a lot that one can learn from them. From the years that they have been in operation, there are certain things that you can pick from the given company. It has experienced a series of phases that can be helpful in identifying if it is a worthy investment. For instance, there are certain companies that have managed to build a recognizable brand. Some of these companies are known not only locally, but also globally. You can narrow down to some 5-10 companies that you would like to invest in, and start evaluating the history of each at a time. Based on your findings, you can settle on the one that you are more comfortable about and have the potential of providing you with future gains. There are some companies that have a reputation for increasing their dividends and paying in time. As you conduct your analysis, you might discover some reputed companies that generate high revenue but fail to increase their dividends. Some might increase them at slight percentages that do not make any big difference. Still, you might discover some that fail to pay on time. Such incidences prove that despite some companies generating huge profits, it may not be a guarantee that they are the best companies to invest in. This brings the need to properly learn the history of a company before engaging in it. The idea is to get an investment that generates an increasing dividend and one that has a history of paying investors. With such, you can rest knowing that your investment is in good hands.

The Potential of the Company

We live in a competitive world whereby one is either outdone or manages to hold their position in the game. In the business sector, competition never ends. You find that there are many companies producing the same product in the same market. Interestingly, despite the similarity in the products, some companies are doing better than others. What results in the difference in capital gain? Well, there are numerous factors that influence the success of any business. Some of these factors I have mentioned while explaining different things in the book. When the product is the same, the company has to come up with different ways of delivering its product to its consumers. For instance, the company could decide to invest in packaging.

There are some people that only purchase a product because it has been made in a way that they like, and it's pleasing to their eyes. Some consumers will get the product because of how it is packaged. You will be surprised to find that some do not buy due to the price. To them, it may appear so cheap for their status. So, a company that invests in packaging can get clients that value quality. They understand that the product is similar to the one being sold at $7, but they want to go for the one retailing at $29. This narrows down to the four p's of marketing and how they influence the profits generated by the company.

Since the product is the same, we will consider the other p's which are; place, promotion, and price. Under place, the location of the company will affect the prices it gives for its product. In this case, we can use a hotel as a perfect example. Hotels that are situated in high-end places tend to have high prices for the services and products that they offer. At the end of the day, they generate more revenue than other hotels in different places. Some invest in promotion as a way to build and establish their brand to their preferred position and point. This allows them to connect with more people and hence earning more than other brands. The potential of a brand can be identified from studying its marketing strategy and the management it has at that given time. These are some factors that can help you know if you can invest in their dividend stocks. We have had some companies that are newly established and managed to get into the market at a fast rate. Within a year or two, they might be in the position of other companies that have been in the industry for long. When you discover the companies that are promising or the ones that have already established a brand, you can feel free to invest in such. They can guarantee that your investment will have the potential of generating an income and that you will leap where you sow.

The Financial Status of the Company

One of the best times to purchase dividend stocks is when the company is in its peak in terms of finances. As an investor, you want to put your money in a place that it can encounter growth. A well-established company with a healthy financial situation can help you achieve such a dream. One can find out more about the financial status of the company by going through their reports. Some of these reports are available online or in magazines produced by the given companies. Earlier on, I stated that not all companies generating high revenue have the potential of generating high income on dividend stocks. This prompts the need to do further research on the companies before making any investment with them. You find that the companies that generate high revenue have the potential of paying higher dividends on stocks. Finding such a company can end up being a real gold mine for any investor. On the other hand, you will come across companies that are not really established, but they have the potential to grow. Such companies can be good to invest in. There are certain factors that will influence the productivity of such companies. When they manage to remain consistent at what they do, they will get to places that they would not have imagined to be in. Sometimes we fail to engage with such since we are uncertain of the directions that they will take. However, it is important that we find out more about the potential of growth and as we decide to invest. There are certain pointers that can encourage one to engage in a given investment. Judging from the direction that the company has been moving towards over the years, you can easily identify if it is fit for you.

The Income and Growth

The growth of a company is essential in ensuring that it has the potential to result in higher returns. As an investor, you want to invest in something that has the potential of bringing returns that you can enjoy. The growth of a company can be influenced by factors such as; offering quality products and services, good public relations and marketing strategy, and proper financial management, among others. The leadership present can also have a big impact on the growth of a company. With growth, it is possible to predict how it will occur. We can use an example of a plant that is developing. As we harvest, we get different produce depending on how the plant grew and what we did to facilitate its growth. There are some plants that turn out to be healthy and perfect for selling, and at the same time, there are others that look unhealthy and barely sell. All these differences are caused by the various factors influencing their growth. As a farmer, one of the key factors you will consider before farming is the type of land you intend to farm on. It has to be fertile and suitable for the plant that you wish to cultivate. Once you plant, you need to apply certain measures that make the situation favorable for the crop to survive and flourish. When some threatening factors crop up, such as weeds and diseases, you have to come up with ways to prevent them.

How does the farming concept relate to dividend stocks? This might be the question that is currently running through your mind. Well, I assume that the product can be equated with the dividend stocks. As a company is nurtured and grows, there are certain results that we expect from the growth incurred. Some of the indicators that a company is doing well are the revenue it generates, the salaries given to the workers, and the dividends given to its investors. As well established and the developing company has the potential paying high dividends. There are certain phases whereby a company experiences sudden capital gain. It later happens that all the things take a wrong turn causing the collapse of a company. At times it is not always right to purchase dividend stocks when the profits have suddenly increased. Things may go wrong that may result in the fall of the company. You need to be extremely careful when making any investment decision since anything that you decide will determine if you will earn a fortune from your investment or if it will be a waste of your resources. A sudden increase in revenue may seem all appealing, but get to understand if the company can sustain that for long or if it is a one-time thing. Once you have done your research, you can determine if it's good for you to invest in the company or if you should avoid it.

Current Dividend

As you evaluate different companies to decide if you will invest in them, consider looking at their current dividends. Companies with a good track record of giving their investors good dividends are likely to do so in the future. Such a company is perfect for investing in since it guarantees a constant potential flow in dividends. With such companies, you can have your dividends increase over the years. The dividends offered by different companies differ depending on the revenue generated by the company and its policies. As mentioned earlier, there are some that will generate high revenue and still give dividends that are not favorable, and at the same time, you will come across some that are friendly in terms of their dividends. All these things are discovered while carrying out your research on the different companies. Well established companies manage to sustain their income as they have come up with ways in which they can stay in the game. In the search for the best dividend stocks to invest in, such companies have always topped the list of most investors. Ideally, one looks for a secure investment that can bring returns. Knowing or discovering a company that can guarantee such returns is one of the best things that can happen to an investor. The best time to acquire dividend stocks is when a company has a constant offer on dividends. Once it has reached this point, you are assured of big returns in the future and are certain of making the right investment

All the above factors are essential while deciding on the best time to buy dividend stocks. One of the emphases I have made in the different points given is focusing on research. There are many things that you might not know, and hence you get to learn them along the way. Having the right information is essential in accomplishing anything in life. While at it, learn that the process of gaining knowledge never stops. We live in a world that id full of discoveries. There is always something new to be learned and discovered. At the same time, we explore different things from different dimensions hoping to make a change in our lives and making it worthwhile. Such principles apply in all aspects of our lives and help us make a difference in what we do. The majority of the mistakes we make are caused by the fact that we never took the time to learn and gain the required information. This ends us in rants of 'I wish I knew,' yet it was something that could have been prevented if we took the time to learn more. To avoid such incidences from occurring, it would be if we conduct proper research on everything that we do. In this case, get to look at all the information necessary before engaging in any dividend stock. Having the right information allows you to make the right decisions, and as a result, you also get excellent returns from your investment.

Chapter 8: The Best Time to Sell Dividend Stocks

The Best Time to Sell Dividend Stocks

One of the hardest things to do as a trader is selling Stock. This is because, as human beings, we end up getting emotionally tied to our Stock, and it gets hard to let go. Coupled with the stubborn mind that refuses to admit how wrong a move was and the tough decision of either fight or flight, most traders end up letting their losers drag on, making the performance of the portfolio worse.

Before we delve into the particulars of when to sell and when to hold, it is imperative that we understand the preparations we need to make before either move. The first thing we have to remember is that prices in the markets will always be volatile. We are prone to emotional fluctuations whenever our investments are either doing too well or not doing well enough. Traders must learn to deal with these changes in a rational and pragmatic manner. Emotions such as overconfidence should not come into play at any given time during trading. Always keep in mind that decisions made on stocks are based on incomplete information and a gamble since no one can ever predict the future. Therefore, as a trader, a more flexible approach is best as a tactical move whenever trading.

This implores the trader to fight the natural instinct of flight or fight and instead hold their ground even if; the mind offers a corrective measure to a move in market prices. Research has shown a number of traders who sell and buy actively make up the majority of losers in the daily activities of the markets. To help you make the right decision on when to hold on to Stock or sell, we have outlined five rules to consider.

Rule 1: Unsteady Long-Term Earnings

As long as a company has a high return of profits, the continuity of the business is assured. How well it performs on a daily basis or weekly basis is not as important as how well the company will do over a period of time. Markets too have bad days, the dividends may perform awfully on the charts, but over time the performance may end up being very lucrative. However, if the earnings of a company fall, this implies the continuity plan of the company is at peril and is a first indicator to the trader.

However, before dropping the ax, the trader should investigate the reason for the change in the earnings. Some reasons are easy to rectify in a few years; these reasons include slow growth of the economy or financial headwinds. Reasons such as a change in consumer preferences, high competition from other companies or countries are hard to overcome, on the other hand, thus making them an easy indication of when to sell dividends.

Rule 2: Excessive levels in Stock Valuation

Fundamentals of a company include sales, debt, and cash flow, which all play an important role in the realization of profits, which in turn influence the position of the Stock in markets. If these fundamentals seem to plummet, the reason may be attributed to something that will have a negative impact on the price of the Stock. Once this indicator appears, the traders should seriously consider selling and gaining from the profit they have already accumulated.

Rule 3: Risk Mitigation

One of the most vital trading rules is that a trader should not invest above a certain percentage in one single company. If the size of Stock that one is currently holding exceeds the portion that the trader is comfortable managing, the trader should consider selling and mitigating the risk that comes with putting all the eggs in one basket. Successful traders should have diverse portfolios that spread risks across various trades and to reduce the pressure on the tolerance for risk in their investment portfolios.

Rule 4: Greener Pastures

A trader may see an opportunity to buy into a stock with higher returns and a better long-term picture, which implies safer dividends. Traders may then sell off the like warm stocks in their baskets and buy into the better and more lucrative Stock, which appears to have better quality and efficiency in business.

Rule 5: Dividend Payment at Risk

A dividend that seems to be growing is considered a clear sign of a business that is healthy and has higher yields. Therefore, the more lucrative the dividend seems, the higher the expectations with some looking forward to high passive incomes. The analysis of debt levels, earnings growth, payout metrics, and other financial metrics can give the trader a picture of the well-being of a company and if there is any reduction that may be applied to the dividend cuts. When the indicators are positive, traders are advised to sell their stocks before this cut is applied.

Other than paying attention to these rules, there are warning signs that a trader should be on the look-out for when trading dividends. Some of these signs include:

Sign 1: Deteriorating Cash Flow

The ability of a company to pay its dividend is determined majorly by the position of the company in the financial books. If the books are healthy and the returns are high, then the ability to pay is equally high. If the company is unable to get a steady cash flow or it's taking huge loans plunging itself in debt, then the ability to pay off dividends is getting crippled too. Traders should pay attention to the company's balance sheets that give a clear image of the assets and liabilities of a company, which help one to figure out if the company is able to generate cash flow that will, in turn, be translated into paying off dividends. If the answers are negative, it is high time to sell the dividends before the loss train strikes.

Sign 2: Downgrades in Credit

A credit downgrade is a cut to the credit rating of a company. This happens when security has had a negative rate changing. Securities are rated and assigned a letter to grade them into categories if security moves from a letter A to a "BBB" rating; this is considered a credit downgrade. A credit downgrade is usually caused by changes in the company's operations either in fundamentals or technical running such as changes in the markets, entry of competition in the line of business that the company operates in, and constricted cash flow. These changes have analysts feeling as though the performance of the securities is not at par with the expectations, or the prospective future is bleak.

This slash to the credit rating implies higher costs when the company issues a new debt, which in turn leads to the changes in the credit rating of the company. To cover for the changes in cash flow, most companies will cut down on their dividends, having the traders suffer most. Whenever a trader spots such a sign, they should consider selling the stock immediately.

Sign 3: Weak Fundamentals

In the rules above, we briefly touched on the fundamentals of a business and how their position is likely to affect the stand of a trader. The stronger the fundamentals of a business are, the stronger the earnings and the better the continuity plan of the business. Therefore, the company can pay dividends back using the sales growth and improve their standing on cash flow by using their earnings growth. Should a company face a challenge in their activities, they find ways to free up cash by either eliminating buyback programs or slashing their dividends anything to have a better cash flow and to ensure the running of the business. Once these signs appear, traders are required to consider selling off their Stock in order to cut down on their losses. It is crucial for a trader to remember that no matter how consistent a trader is in paying dividends or increasing the payment, their main concern is the cash flow and the continuity of a business.

Sign 4: Suspension of Stock Buyback Programs

In the previous paragraph, we have explained the reasons why the company would suspend the buyback programs. With all that in mind, a successful trader will always know that the second move for the company will be to cut down on dividends, and they will strive to find a way to get out of the trade before this move is made.

In the wake of low-interest rates on stocks, the decrease in traders has been major, to curb this, companies have adopted a strategy which is known as stock buyback. The companies fund the aggressive buying back programs by introducing cheap debt that leads to an increase in the value of shares. This is cut down whenever the company goes into debt or has a go-slow in their cash flow.

Sign 5: Fall in the stock prices

Whenever a company faces issues with money before cutting down on dividends, they first reallocate the money in the budget and find some way to pay the dividend payments. In case the company moves money around, and it still isn't enough to pay the dividends, the firm will likely go into debt and borrow money to cover these costs or sell off some shares to make more money. One of the effects of these actions is the increase in dividend yields. Investors should be cautious once a corporation has high dividend yields and falling prices in the market. Because the moment the company cuts down on its dividends because of the shortage in cash flow, the investors will get into trouble caused by hefty losses.

One of the major problems traders fail is timing the exit in whatever wave they are riding on the charts. Most investors make money on a trade and lose a portion of the profits because of the awful timing on the exit. The emotion fluctuations caused by the movements of the markets and price fluctuations contribute majorly to these losses that are incurred. To avoid such losses, traders are advised to conduct thorough technical analysis and to be vigilant and on the look-out for the signs that have been discussed above. Beyond being vigilant, the trader should also ensure they make a trading plan that takes into consideration the time frame that trading is taking place; a long-term investment plan is likely to yield more gains than a short-term active trading strategy.

Finally, traders should also pay close attention to the legal policies governing a nation and the corporation they have invested in. Simple changes in legislation can trigger a major loss in the market, a good example of such a policy was the vote for Brexit which led to major changes and price fluctuations in firms and the markets.

It is important always to remember the main rule of trading whether it is in Forex, Stock, Options, Futures, or dividends is "Profits are the first priority," with this rule in mind, traders are guaranteed to cut down on losses and gain more profits. Traders who keep this rule in mind will always be on the look-out for the slightest sign of trouble and exit whenever they feel their positions are under threat. I urge you to embrace this approach as well to maximize your returns.

Chapter 9: How to Create A Passive Income with Dividend Stocks

How to Create a Passive Income with Dividend Stocks

Passive income can be defined as money that you regularly earn without having actually to put in much effort in order to gain. It is mostly associated with dividends, rents, or interests. Investors trade with the idea of making enough money in the future when they no longer have a paycheck to support their lifestyles as their income. Before embarking on the journey of making the most out of passive income in dividend stock trading, it is important for the trader to keep a few warnings at the back of their minds.

Warning 1: The Key Is Patience

It takes time to build a good portfolio that will generate more yields that will exceed the inflation rate. Traders require to build their own investment portfolios that will give them more returns over time. Getting this portfolio right is a hassle that will require a few mistakes, losses, small wins before eventually getting the bucks from the big wins? It may help if the trader remembers that Rome, too, was not built in a single day.

Warning 2: Avoid the Trap

The dividend trap is seen whenever the prices of the Stock are falling, but the dividend earnings are not falling as well too. The majority of the young investors who are hungry for profits get suckered into this sweet deal and suffer losses before they can get themselves disentangled from the trap of the values. One of the general rules that every trader must consider to avoid getting caught in this trap is "Avoid Cheap Assets" some assets will give returns that are about three or four times greater than the Treasury Bond. As a trader, it is imperative for one to be cautious when you stumble upon such instruments. Every instrument that is considered cheap has a reason behind the "cheapness," and more often than not, this cheap turns out to be very expensive. This applies to dividends that have percentages that are above 6 percent on their returns. Some of the reasons why a company would have such high returns include but are not limited to:

1. The company receives a huge paycheck for the disposal of an asset, maybe a subsidiary which resulted in the fat dividend checks - which was a onetime thing that the company will most likely not achieve again in a while
2. The firm receives a hefty paycheck in settlement of a lawsuit that sees them also give a hefty check to the dividend holders of the firm. A feat the company is likely never to achieve again
3. It could also be a stroke of luck in the market, and a certain commodity reaches a record high price and brings in revenue that the management also shares with the shareholders by giving them a hefty paycheck.

The similarity between the three reasons is, a hefty paycheck paid into the company once can alter the known planes of the dividend fields and tilt it all in a favored direction. The lack of a continued chance to earn this kind of profit will not make a huge difference in what the books say about the dividends, and any firm can ride out this wave as long as they can in order to lure in unsuspecting shareholders who will increase the cash flow and get little returns for their investments.

With these warnings in mind, it is now the right time for the trader to make a good investment portfolio and the first question the trader must tackle is;

How Much Money Do You Need to Startup?

This question is the most common question on every investor's lips once a business idea is pitched. For dividend stock trading, the investor makes a move depending on their normal spending and cost habits. It is imperative for a trader to calculate how much money they spend throughout an entire year before they make the decision on how much money they need to set aside for saving. The higher the amount they spend is, the higher the amount they need to save as well for the future.

Let us assume that you need to spend about 60 000 US Dollars a year for you to lead a comfortable life presently. The most common mistake traders make building a portfolio that gives high returns without necessarily paying attention to the risk this portfolio attracts. It is advisable to hold on to a portfolio that is more diverse and less prone to risk. For example, a portfolio that gives returns of 20% but more prone to risk may look attractive, but a more diverse portfolio with a 7% return is a better choice.

In order to live off passive income, the trader is required to hold on to a portfolio that has a million US Dollars' worth of Stock. That will most likely discourage you from this business because saving a million seems like an impossible task. However, little by little, your portfolio will achieve this status and surpass it if you make a good and informed choice. To get this portfolio, you need to save at least fifty thousand US Dollars in a year and invest it in diverse Stock. The stock market has a return that is above 12% every year, with the right decisions in twenty years you will achieve a portfolio of a million and the dividend returns will be enough for you to live off the passive income that you will earn.

The easiest way of making this process faster is by re-investing what you have earned. The second question that you need to tackle as a trader is;

How Do I Know What the Right Stock Is?

Now that we are aware of the amount of money, we need to get a good income to live off. It is imperative that we know the right Stock to have in our portfolio in order to make our dreams possible with little or no mishaps along the journey.

The first thing to keep in mind is never buying Stock that you cannot keep for at least ten years. This means you need to carry out extensive research on everything about the company, including their history, their future aspirations, and current state, both managerial and financial before making the decision to invest in a company and add it to your portfolio. It is safer to invest in the different sectors of the economy and maybe different companies in different geographical locations. The best thing about this kind of research, the internet has provided easy access to information about companies, and some websites provide information about the good dividend stock to invest in for free.

The second thing to do is finding the right brokerage firm that will not charge you exorbitant fees as commissions or end up being unreliable. Commission fees will eat away at your profits and slow down your journey to achieving the right portfolio in the shortest time.

Once you have a stockbroker in mind, it is important to know the calculations that are done by every trader in order to maximize every shilling you invest in the markets. This will help the trader in the allocation of the portfolio and dividing it, making it a diverse and attractive portfolio.

How to Effectively Allocate the Dividend Portfolio

The dividends are divided into aristocrats and kings. These are the major players you want in your consumer index basket. Dividend Aristocrats are all the firms that have a proven track record of being consistent in their dividend payouts to the shareholders for at least twenty-five years and also end up increasing the amount of money they pay to the dividend holders. This is a company that will not surprise their consumers with news of bankruptcy or estranged cash flow levels and also very expensive yields. This also means getting the Stock in such companies is pricy but a worthy investment.

Dividend kings, on the other hand, are companies that have a proven track record of being consistent in their dividend payouts to the shareholders for at least fifty consecutive years with an increment of the value over time. The difference between dividend aristocrats and dividend kings is the growth rate. Kings have a slow but steady growth rate, which makes them a greater success, while aristocrats have a faster growth rate. The smart move for a successful trader is to incorporate different values of every dividend. In my opinion, the best portfolio would have:

1. At least twenty percent of Dividend kings
2. At least thirty-five percent of Dividend Aristocrats
3. At least thirty percent of dividend stocks that are consistent but not yet in the kings or aristocrat's classification. This includes any dividend stock that has a proven track record of paying their dividends and increasing the payouts. They are considered to be in line to be aristocrats.
4. Finally, your dividend growth portfolio should have at least fifteen percent of dividend growth stocks that are in the global dividend growth fund. These are usually international companies that are considered blue chips.

This diversification should mean your investment portfolio has more than 20 companies that are likely to perform well over a period of time. After investing in this growing portfolio, it is advisable for the trader to re-invest back in their own portfolio so that the dividends can be higher in the future. As you track your portfolio and build it into the desired basket for a retirement package, it is vital to learn the essential things you need to calculate. They include:

1. **Annual Dividend Yield:** this is a comparison of the percentage of the dividend per share that was received to the stock price. This shows how much the investor will get once they invest in a certain stock for a period of twelve months. An

investor with the intention of living off passive income will only be safe if the result of this comparison shows that the yields received over a period of twelve months is as high as it can be as compared to the cost of buying the shares.

2. **Dividend Growth Rate:** this is calculated by dividing the dividend per share of the previous year by the dividend share of the current year and subtracting one from this answer. The importance of the dividend growth rate is it portrays the growth rate of the firm in general. The other good thing about this is; the trader gets a consistent rise in their income, and in a real sense, all they did was pay some cash to a firm- this could be considered a raise for doing nothing. Passive income traders will want this rate to be as high as it can get.

3. **Dividend Payout Ratio:** this is calculated by measuring the amount that is paid out as dividends and comparing it to the price of the earnings. The higher this ratio is, the louder the warning and the greater the risks. Since this implies that the firm is keeping a certain amount of cash for reinvestment in its own self, this further translates that, the moment the earnings the company earns falls short, there will have to be a decrease in the cut of dividend payout for the dividend stock. And ever passive income investor would rather have a dividend stock that assures them of paying out a dividend and increasing the amount over a period of time no matter what wave rocks their boats.

With all this information at hand, you are now ready to invest in dividends with the aim of living off passive income. Although first, you have to contribute a certain amount per month to the portfolio in the fastest way possible. The higher this amount is, the better for you as a trader. Then after twelve months, consider increasing your monthly contributions by about twenty-five percent per annum. The first ten years of this process have been documented as the easiest part of the journey after the tenth year; things reportedly get harder but manageable. Once you have determined the contributions, you make to the portfolio, re-invest every profit you make off your basket. Beware of the dividend reinvestment plan, which automatically buys back into the same Stock. Instead, opt for the option that you can use the earnings to whatever Stock you find suitable at that specific moment. Keep in mind that you need to buy Stock that is considered of quality such that you can have a growth rate of about six percent in your equity value. That means that out of ten stocks, at least six or seven stocks should be making a profit.

Living off dividends is made easy by compound interest computations that lead to a double increase in the value of the portfolio and the income generated by this value appreciation.

Chapter 10: How to Find the Best Dividend Stocks

How to Find the Best Dividend Stocks

To find the best dividend stock, it is imperative to remember that this is a long-term investment process that requires extensive research and analysis of the firms in the portfolios to gain the most out of it. It also requires constant evaluation to contribute to the informed decisions that one needs to make as the years go forth. To avoid making hasty decisions, investors should always avoid a company that is in deep debt. This is because a company that is in a huge debt will have to allocate a certain amount of cash to pay off the debt. This is money that would have otherwise been used to increase the value of dividends for the investor. This means that the investors have to pay attention to the debt to equity ratio of the firms in question. Companies with a high debt to equity ratio should be knocked off the dividend growth portfolio. Since everyone has their own opinion of what a high debt to equity ratio is, there has not been an official conclusion of what exactly the maximum or minimum ratio a company should maintain to avoid high ratios. Although generally, a firm that has a debt to equity ratio that is higher than two are considered to have a high rate. Investors are encouraged to invest in firms that have a debt to equity ratio that is less than 1.00 since this is considered a safer investment.

Investors will also need to pay attention to the health of the industry in general. For instance, industries that are currently facing the boom are likely to increase their dividend payouts since the income promises to be higher and better. This means that the investor should analyze both the past and current situation of the firm and the larger industry it operates in. It is possible for a firm to have had a good past record of paying consistent dividends with an increase over time to do very bad currently, especially if their services are no longer as vital as they used to be. For instance, the Courier services used to be unrivaled in the stock market, and the companies that were listed paid their shareholders attractive dividends that promised growth. Today the same companies are merging together to see if they can make an impact in the world of technology that allows you to send mails through the internet instead of a physical location and courier. This means the cash flow is constricted, and their dividends today are not as attractive as they seemed in the past.

Investors also need to pay attention to the first rule of passive income investing, which is paying close attention to the earnings of the firm. A firm that has very high earning growth expectations will be considered as a high-risk asset that will likely lead to earnings disappointments for the investor. Companies that have a profit deliver good positive dividend payoffs, including those that do not show good growth over a period of time, for example, twelve months. However faced with a decision between a firm that has positive dividend payoffs while showing little or no growth and a firm that has both a positive dividend pay off and growth of the firm in general, the investor is advised to go with the latter since the growth means that the dividends are likely to appreciate in value over time. The best long-term earnings growth expectations rates for a firm should vary between five percent and fifteen percent.

Finally, investors need to ensure the firms can generate their cash flow in a steady manner that will not lead to a shortage of money to pay for dividends. Firms that have a track record of increasing their dividends consistently over a period of time, for example, five years or more, are attractive to investors because they have higher odds when it comes to dividend growth as compared to the other firms. Any stock that lives up to these expectations should be in the investment portfolio of every investor.

How then do you make a choice on what is the best dividend stocks? By doing extensive research as you consider the following factors;

Long-Term Prospects

A passive income investment portfolio is full of Stock that seems to be on track to make a better income minting stock in the market that can translate to high dividends. Investors are not traders, and they do not look to buy stock and sell it later in the markets, they are looking to buy the stock and hold on to it for as long as they want to. This means they must pick firms that seem to have positive long-term prospects despite the numerous economic changes that are scheduled to take place. Although it is not encouraged, dividend investors can sell their stocks in the markets, especially when the aspects of the business change or the strategy no longer seems to stand.

Finances

The balance statement of every firm contains vital information such as ratios, which include but are not limited to; price and sales ratios, debt to equity ratios, price to earnings ratio, and other information such as book value, assets value, liabilities value, and many other. However, the majority of us do not know how to read the traditional balance sheet and, therefore, do not understand what is written and published. For those who cannot understand the balance, you need to pay attention to the bond rating of the company. The bond rating of a company is the letter that is assigned to the bonds to show the credit quality of a bond. The most attractive dividend stock to buy is with the companies that have top-notch credit ratings that are considered either investment grades or higher. Firms with huge debts are also a no-go zone since the creditors are entitled to payment before the shareholders who are holding the dividend stocks scramble for the remaining cash.

Management and Dividend History

Consider companies with a management team that has a soft spot for investors. This means management that has been looking out for their dividend investors by paying their dividends promptly and consistently over time. This involves doing extensive research on the management and their history with dividend stock clients. The questions to ask include:

1. Does the firm pay dividends consistently or periodically?
2. Does the value of dividend payouts increase or decrease over time?
3. Has the management put a break on the dividends scheme?
4. Has the management steered the company in the direction of consistent growth over time?

Competition

How does the industry that your firm is located in doing? Are there any upcoming companies that are likely to put your firm out of business in a couple of years? If the answer to the latter is yes, then that is not Stock that is worth investing since the well will dry up soon. Companies that have been in play for longer periods of time have withstood the test of changing economic times and the pressure to cave in. These companies are the leaders in their own industries and the best to add up in the portfolio. Giving you the most of their returns in the payoffs.

Risk

Most of the factors discussed above are risk assessment theories of the firms in their own capacity. For instance, the cash flow in the business is considered the risk of leverage in the model of the business. The size of the company, which incorporates the staff, the assets, and the liabilities of the company are another risk assessment question that the investor needs to have an answer to. It is a time-consuming process of researching and evaluating how risky a stock that has high dividend returns is, but it is also a very important aspect of finding the right dividend stock. To ease the process, researchers came up with a dividend safety score that goes through financial statements of a company to calculate how safe a dividend payment is and what risk it carries. This process helps eliminate the dividend traps that we mentioned in the previous chapters. The dividend safety score ranges from zero to a hundred. The table below shows how the rating is done.

Dividend Safety Score	81-100	61-80	41-60	21-40	0-20
Rating	Very Safe	Safe	Borderline Safe	Unsafe	Very Unsafe
Translation	Dividends will not be terminated	Dividends are unlikely to be terminated	There is a low risk of dividends being terminated	There is a greater risk of dividends being terminated	Very high risk of the dividends being terminated

From this table, it is evident that investors need to buy into a firm that has a dividend safety score that is at least sixty. The higher the dividend safety score of the Stock is, the more attractive the Stock becomes for the investment growth portfolio.

Ultimately, I believe that the best thing about passive income investment is the ability to earn money without the hassle of constantly "working" for it. It does not come with the instant satisfaction of knowing what one has made or done right or the instant disappointment and loss when one makes a bad move like in the short-term investing strategies. It also gives the investor a higher chance of making more money in the name of steady earnings and incomes as compared to the short-term investing strategies.

Chapter 11: How to Not Overpay for Dividend Stock

How to Not Overpay for Dividend Stock

One of the major problems novice traders face is how to know the actual value of the Stock. Once the other players in the industry realize that you are green in this industry, the likelihood of them taking advantage of you is very high. To avoid these situations; here are a few questions you should ask yourself:

Is the Stock Right for Your Portfolio?

If you have built a portfolio that is diversified and you already have dividend kings worth twenty percent of the portfolio, if you come across another dividend king being sold at the right price, will you buy into it? If your answer was yes, then you are wrong. You should stick to the plan always. The key to a successful trader is being disciplined and sticking to the right plan instead of going with the wave. Instead of investing in the dividend king, you should instead invest in the securities that are not enough in your portfolio.

How Solid Are the Fundamentals of the Stock?

Fundamental analysis has been discussed in the first part of this book, but in case the other information in between has made you forget the definition here it is once more. Fundamental analysis is the aspect of going through the financial statements of the firm one is interested in and analyzing each of the figures in order to get a clear image of where exactly the firm stands. Is the ground their foundation is built on strong or shaky? This will help the trader or investor in making the decision on how fast the company is growing both in terms of size and the earnings (revenue). It also paints a picture of the management and their relationship with the rest of the stakeholders.

How Does the Stock Perform Against the Competition?

If you are given a choice between Coca-Cola and an upcoming soda company, whose stock is performing better than the other? The obvious answer is Coca-Cola is performing better than the other company. This is because, as a global company that has been in the market for decades. Investors have analyzed and proved their track record is good. This is the beauty of a strong brand name, which gives the company an edge over all its competitors or their less-known counterparts.

How Reasonable Is the Price for the Stock?

Pay attention to the prices that other investors are paying for the Stock that you are interested in. It is bad to pay an extra amount for a certain stock, whether it is a good company or a bad performing company. However, the price tag of Stock is not the measure of how reasonable the price is. A firm that sells one share at twenty dollars could be more expensive to buy into than a firm that sells its shares at fifty dollars per share.

How is this possible? If the company that sells at twenty dollars per share has low earning attached to each share, for instance, a return of one dollar per share and you bought a hundred shares of this means, you are getting back a hundred dollars after spending two thousand dollars to buy into the company. The second company that sold its shares at fifty shillings per share has a return of ten dollars per share. This means out of a hundred shares; you will record a return of a thousand dollars after spending five thousand to buy into the company. In the long run –that is five years you will have made your own capital back, in this case, assuming there is no dividend raise while it will take you a whopping ten years to make your own capital back in the other scenario. By then, the investor who bought the fifty-dollar stock will have made a profit of the same amount they invested in assuming they do not re-invest their earnings or get a raise.

However, we cannot blame most of the traders for the mistakes they make since most of them grasp at straws when they are thrown in the world of financial markets all at once. Below we will point out some of the reasons why traders fall into the trap of paying too much for a stock.

Lack of Basic Know-How

I have never taken the time to understand the fundamentals.

The cause traders miss cash is because they forgot to know the correct foundations of how the stock market operates in their struggle to get trading. Get to know the stock market, some trading methods, and get plenty of paper trading exercise. Any information that you acquire will make your likelihood of achievement better.

Lack of Savings

Do not need to have a considerable deposit to begin trading, contrary to a common faith. However, as your business expands, you need to be intelligent about what you are doing with your cash. If you burn your income every moment you create money, you will never enhance your business place. You will be home to ground zero if you gain $8,000 on trade and immediately break it down. Smart traders see the large image and save a nice part of their earnings to enhance their situation over the moment gradually. They can boost their assets progressively. This usually matches their developing skills as traders beautifully. These tiny victories slowly start to match up over the moment.

Lack of Proper Research

The process of creating a trade requires real times, study, and preparing into a trade can extend hours, days, or even decades of surveillance and monitoring. Trading is a play of figures, and using previous data to create choices for the future is one of the keys to achievement. Looking at how it took place in the past, you can start doing business from a location of more excellent safety and trust.

Prospective businesses and scanning the industry with an instrument is essential. This study will often disclose data that will assist you in identifying whether or not at this specific moment a specific trade is a good idea.

Lack of Proper Guidance

Courses on daytime and/or a mentor are crucial to assisting fresh traders in succeeding. Classes can assist new traders in discovering not only the foundations but also experience distinct techniques of trading, which can help them in creating a range from which to start forging their own distinctive fashion. Another major is a mentor.

Lack of a Trading Journal

You develop as a trader; you will advance through many techniques that function, and some that do not work. Just as much as you believe you understand precisely what is going on, the only moment can really inform you. By entering in every trading day, including what you have done, how you feel, and the outcomes, you will receive a strong understanding of the techniques and procedures that really serve your profession. This will allow you to concentrate on what works and reject what is not.

Fear of Failure

A prevalent occurrence as to why traders are losing cash is that they are too scared to make a loss. They are so afraid to lose some money that they follow only trades and deals that bring minimal danger. Although you should never be dangerous, you will have to move out a little bit of your comfort zone. To see benefits, you must embrace a certain amount of danger–or at least become familiar with it. The stock market is an intrinsic risk. One of the most potent methods to mitigate this, however, is to teach you and study extensively. This is the distinction between danger and calculated danger, and you can be more confident in your trade.

It is never a stage where learning stops when you are a trader. You always need to be at the tip of your toes. For example, with a certain method, Joe, the trader becomes relaxed and just starts doing it, not holding a record of how the industry is moving. He becomes careless about their studies, and screening is not so cautious. He is bound to start losing cash after a while. Complacency is a common justification for losing cash to traders. You will probably start wasting over the moment when you stagnate as a trader. Never become idle in your studies, and never suppose that anything could land as a sure bet. Approach each trade as though it were your first, and look at it from every angle.

Chapter 12: Building and Diversifying an Investment Portfolio

Building and Diversifying an Investment Portfolio

A good portfolio has to have stock that is spread out in order for the risk to be spread across the different industries and geographical locations if possible. This means that the portfolio will earn a very high return on the various stock and the least potential risk. Capital will always react differently to the same economic change, for instance, the announcement of Brexit led to a plunge in prices for inventory that was located in the United Kingdom, but it led to a boom in the stock of firms located in the United States of America. If you had both dividend stocks in your growing portfolio, you either gained from the increase in the USA or ended up breaking even. Either way, the risk was controlled and dealt with, unlike an investor whose portfolio was full of Blue-Chip companies that are located in the United Kingdom. To avoid this mess, here are tips to help you in the journey of diversification.

Spread Your Wealth

Heed the advice; do not put all your eggs in one basket. We cannot stress this point enough for everyone to understand what exactly it means. Think of it as investing in mutual funds that you have created for your own personal gratification. Spread your wings and invest in the international companies as well as the local companies you know. However, do not stretch yourself beyond limits. Do not pay to have a portfolio that has over fifty firms in the name of diversification. This large number will have you straining to carry out periodical research in a bid to keep up with the current economic changes and future prospects. A manageable portfolio should have at least twenty to thirty stocks from different investments. An example of a good collection will have:

1. At least twenty percent of Dividend kings
2. At least thirty-five percent of Dividend Aristocrats
3. At least thirty percent of dividend stocks that are consistent but not yet in the kings or aristocrats classification. This includes any dividend stock that has a proven track record of paying their dividends and increasing the payouts. They are considered to be in line to be aristocrats.
4. Finally, your dividend growth portfolio should have at least fifteen percent of dividend growth stocks that are in the global dividend growth fund. These are usually international companies that are considered blue chips.

Reinvest in Your Portfolio

It is essential to reinvest back in your portfolio. The best time to make a good portfolio is the present moment. This is because the younger you are and with a steady income, the easier it will be to pump cash into the wallet and build a good retirement package. The second advantage of building up a portfolio is creating a safe haven that will help smooth out the fluctuations of market and price volatility. This also gives one money to spend when opportunities such as low prices of stocks are made available.

Have an Exit Strategy

One of the mistakes traders and investors make is holding on to a stock that is not performing as well as expected. Simply because dividend investing does not require one to buy with the aim of selling does not mean that one should stick through it all, even when they are bound to make losses. If a stock is having the negative effects on your stock portfolio, consider cutting it off as soon as possible. It is important to get the right timing since, at times, the darkest hour is known to come right before dawn. The only way to avoid making errors that you will regret, such as not cashing into big paychecks, is by staying at par with the current economic changes across the globe and especially in the industry and location that the companies you have invested in are operating from. This will give you a vivid picture of what to expect, what influences the changes, thereby providing a perfect opportunity for the trader or investor to get off the bandwagon when these questions paint a bleak picture of the future.

Be Aware of the Different Charges You Incur

Another common error made by investors and traders is failing to factor in charges that will eat away at the money in the accounts such as commissions charged by brokerage firms or taxation and legislation cuts by the government on the firms that they choose to invest in. It is also important for one to understand why they pay the fees to the account holders and brokers. Some fees are only paid by those who do active trading; these are usually monthly fees while passive traders are charged in a more subtle manner. This does not mean that you should opt for accounts that do not have so many charges or expensive cuts; at times, cheap can get very expensive. At the end of the day, as long as you fully understand why you are being charged for anything, you will stop feeling like you are being robbed in broad daylight.

The bottom line is, you need to adopt a very strict and disciplined approach in any trading you do. Whatever strategy you choose to adopt, ensure you are fully aware of what is required of you and what exactly you get from the strategy. With this information at hand, investing for you should be an easy walk across the park with attractive rewards.

It is imperative to remember that this is a long-term investment process that requires extensive research and analysis of the firms in the portfolios to gain the most out of it.

It also requires constant evaluation to contribute to the informed decisions that one needs to make as the years go forth.

To avoid making hasty decisions, investors should always avoid a company that is in deep debt. This is because a company that is in a huge debt will have to allocate a certain amount of cash to pay off the debt. This is money that would have otherwise been used to increase the value of dividends for the investor.

This means that the investors have to pay attention to the debt to equity ratio of the firms in question. Companies with a high debt to equity ratio should be knocked off the dividend growth portfolio. Since everyone has their own opinion of what a high debt to equity ratio is, there has not been an official conclusion of what exactly the maximum or minimum ratio a company should maintain to avoid high ratios.

Investors will also need to pay attention to the health of the industry in general.

Investors also need to pay attention to the first rule of passive income investing, which is paying close attention to the earnings of the firm. A firm that has very high earning growth expectations will be considered as a high-risk asset that will likely lead to earnings disappointments for the investor. Companies that have a profit deliver good positive dividend payoffs, including those that do not show good growth over a period of time, for example, twelve months. However faced with a decision between a firm that has positive dividend payoffs while showing little or no growth and a firm that has both a positive dividend pay off and growth of the firm in general, the investor is advised to go with the latter since the growth means that the dividends are likely to appreciate in value over time. The best long-term earnings growth expectations rates for a firm should vary between five percent and fifteen percent.

Finally, investors need to ensure the firms can generate their cash flow in a steady manner that will not lead to a shortage of money to pay for dividends. Firms that have a track record of increasing their dividends consistently over a period of time, for example, five years or more, are attractive to investors because they have higher odds when it comes to dividend growth as compared to the other firms. Any stock that lives up to these expectations should be in the investment portfolio of every investor.

One of the major benefits of diversification of portfolios is the spreading of risk. While this may be hard to do, especially for a trader that has never before diversified their own portfolio, it is important to pick the right broker to help in this decision making. The second thing to do is finding the right brokerage firm that will not charge you exorbitant fees as commissions or end up being unreliable. Commission fees will eat away at your profits and slow down your journey to achieving the right portfolio in the shortest time.

Once you have a stockbroker in mind, it is important to know the calculations that are done by every trader in order to maximize every shilling you invest in the markets. This will help the trader in the allocation of the portfolio and dividing it, making it a diverse and attractive portfolio.

How to Select a Stockbroker

The following guidelines are to help you choose the best stockbroker.

Regulation

Any time you decide to join stock trading, you will only have a peaceful night if you are confident that the stockbroker you are working with is being regulated somewhere. Broker's regulations differ from one country to the other, so you need to make sure that you get one from your country.

Execution

You will always want to check out how your broker executes your trade. Pay attention to how the spreads move out before significant release.

Customer Service

There are those times that you are wondering why this happened, and you want to talk to someone who can offer you explanations. These explanations can be through email, and you don't want to wait like forever for your answer. Remember, customer service should not be one that wants to brush you away.

Ease of Withdrawal

Once you have made your money, you will need to withdraw some. You will never want to choose a broker who will offer you an excuse for why you can't withdraw your money when you need it. Be it based on bank issues or technical issues. The best that you are looking for is to get your money within five working days. Thus, your broker has no reason or excuses why your money is delayed.

How to Protect Yourself from Your Brokers

There are those that you realize that the fault wasn't yours hence the need to protect yourself. M, maybe you have been stopped out of your trade. The following are some of the tips that can help you defend yourself against your brokers.

Record and Screen Capture Everything

Record everything by screen-capturing your chats, the level that you entered, the price that you got hit out of your stock. Again, you need to record the cost of another broker. Let us say that the price from these two brokers is different, so this can help you argue your case out. Once you have captured all this information and you are sure that you have no-fault, you can go and share it out on social media. However, you need to ask your broker first for an explanation before sharing this with social media. If you dint get a certificatory reason, then you are free to share it out to social media. This may break your broker's reputation as it will be shared worldwide. The chances are that your broker may try to make amends, and thus they may refund you whatever losses that you incurred. You can share this on your Facebook wall or the Facebook group. People will help you share this. After all, they all think that they are all on this together.

If you don't want to share your uncertainty on social media, you can bring it out to the authorities. The regulators will impose a fee to the broker. This is a cost to the broker whether they did something wrong or not. Thus, the broker may decide to waiver the loss incurred instead of paying the regulation fee.

With the right broker in mind and their sound advice readily available, you should now consider what stock to buy in to. The first thing to keep in mind is never buying a stock that you cannot keep for at least ten years. This means you need to carry out extensive research on everything about the company, including their history, their future aspirations, and current state, both managerial and financial, before making the decision to invest in a company and add it to your portfolio. It is safer to invest in the different sectors of the economy and maybe different companies in different geographical locations. The best thing about this kind of research, the internet has provided easy access to information about companies, and some websites provide information about the good dividend stock to invest in for free.

PART THREE:
Success Tips

The above parts of the book have given you all the basic information you need to indulge in dividend portfolio trading. In this last part of the book, we will learn about the important tips to be a successful dividend stock investor. The first step will have you learning about the common mistakes that most investors do that rob them off millions in their portfolios sugarcoated and named losses by the elite. We will also learn the importance of aspects such as discipline in order to gain an edge above everyone else. The final chapter of this book will help us understand how to succeed while we invest in dividend stocks. We will touch on the different hidden alleys that most traders and investors have no idea exist and how we can maximize on this and earn high earnings. Therefore, brew yourself another pot of coffee, kick back, and enjoy this final part of the book.

Chapter 13: Mistakes People Make While Investing in Dividend Stocks and How to Avoid Them

Mistakes People Make While Investing in Dividend Stocks and How to Avoid Them

The strategy of dividend investing has, over the years, proved to be an asset to investors, especially those with the intention of living off their dividend income in the future. However, the downside to this is the damage that can be caused by an investor if this strategy is not utilized in the right manner. To ensure that you are not up for disaster, we have discussed some of the common mistakes that investors make in dividend investment and added a few remarks on the best way to eradicate the damages caused by these mishaps or how to reduce the effects of these speed bumps.

Finding Dividends in the Wrong Areas

The majority of investors pay attention to the wrong sectors of the economy for their investments. They are drawn by large cheques that are dished out once in a while by companies that seem to be leading in the growth sector; thereby, making the mistake of investing in companies that are focused on growth and not rewarding their investors regularly. For instance, companies in the tech world are in the fastest-growing sector of the industry, making them seem very lucrative for an investor after all technology is here to stay and surprise us by its growth on a daily basis. However, investors fail to realize the amounts of capital these companies require to run their business how periodic these capital investments are. This can constrict the cash flow of tech giants leading to irregular payouts for the dividends. This industry is marred with business strategies that often require a merger of firms or the acquisition of a firm by another. These two activities require a lot of capital, especially if the firm is involved in the acquisition of another company. The nature of how this business is carried out leaves one more speculative than normal, which will also contribute greatly to the fact that the dividends payoffs do not have a reliable future in this industry.

To avoid this mistake, investors are required to conduct an extensive analysis and research of the companies they are interested in, as well as the sector of the economy they operate in. the industry players should be analyzed individually and compared in order for the investor to get a clear picture of what they are getting in to. Some companies have withstood the test of time, and economic changes and these are the ideal company for every investor.

Ignoring Payout Ratios

In the chapters above, we explained how to calculate payout ratios and the importance in depth. As a reminder, payout ratios are calculated by dividend the money that a firm has spent on divided in the previous twelve months by the net income it has earned over a period of twelve months. If the payout ratio is at fifty percent or less, then this is considered a safe investment. A company that is losing money has a payout ratio that is above fifty percent, and a company that is making profits and gaining money has a ratio that is below fifty percent.

Failing to Reinvest Dividend Payments

For a shot at success, it is imperative for the investor to invest in the investment as much as they can either financially or setting time aside. While doing this, the investor needs to either take nothing out or to take as little as they can. Therefore, instead of taking out the entire cheque even when it is higher than the amount you need for your activities between the two payment terms, it is best for you to put the excess cash back into the portfolio for that extra kick that is needed in achieving greater lengths.

Overpaying for the Stock

The human nature of investors is drawn out, and they focus on the growth story of the company and make decisions without paying any particular attention to the measure and ratios such as the price to earnings and price to book values. This drive to seek a high price to earnings ratios will lead to a massive downfall whenever the reality is not at par with the expectations of the investor. On the other hand, a low price to earnings ratio will most likely mean that the business is going under the water. To avoid this, investors need to use ratios such as the dividend ratio, price to earnings, etcetera. However, these should not be the only tools that an investor uses to carry out extensive research.

Using a Dividend Strategy Inappropriately

Most of the traders do not fully grasp the technical and fundamental aspects of strategies for dividend strategies before they choose to use them in their investment plans. This move hurts their portfolios and leaves them in debt or dealing with major losses on their end.

To avoid getting caught in the crossfire, traders need to fully understand the requirements for certain strategies and their own financial ability to venture into the markets. This means having a clear picture of their own financial capabilities by analyzing their own cash flow needs, their assets, liabilities, and how much they can comfortably set aside for dividend stock investment. With this mental image, investors can now pick the appropriate strategies that will not weigh down on them.

Misjudging Personal Financial Status

Living off dividend income is a process that can be achieved over a period of time. Unfortunately, most investors want to rush the process and achieve Warren Buffet's status as soon as they start making their investments. This ambition hurts the finances that they have in store and leaves them grasping at straws because of the debt they find themselves in. When investors have high expectations of the dividend income, they are more prone to making financial decisions that will go beyond the normal stand, which could leave them with a financial crisis when the actual dividend income paycheck arrives. To avoid this, investors should only spend what they have in hand after their other financial needs and also set the bar high for their investment returns so that the odds of the results will be as high as possible.

Flying Alone

It is impossible for any person to live as an island. Successful businessmen have their financial advisors who give a different set of eyes on any business decision that they are about to embrace. In dividend stock investing, investors are also advised to have a different set of eyes on their decisions before they make that final move. It can be a professional advisor who deals with investment portfolios or a close friend who has business acumen. It should be anyone who is not selfish enough to value their own needs above the investors' goals in the trading calendar. Dividend investing has its own complex complications that may be hard for the layman to draw any conclusions from, which is why there are numerous professional advisors readily available on the internet or on the ground to guide the investors in the right moves all the way from the research to the actual investing.

Falling into the Dividend Trap

The dividend trap is seen whenever the prices of the stock are falling, but the dividend earnings are not falling as well too. The majority of the young investors who are hungry for profits get suckered into this sweet deal and suffer losses before they can get themselves disentangled from the trap of the values. One of the general rules that every trader must consider to avoid getting caught in this trap is "Avoid Cheap Assets" some assets will give returns that are about three or four times greater than the Treasury Bond. As a trader, it is imperative for one to be cautious when you stumble upon such instruments. Every instrument that is considered cheap has a reason behind the "cheapness," and more often than not, this cheap turns out to be very expensive. This applies to dividends that have percentages that are above 6 percent on their returns.

Getting into a Panic Frenzy

Most of the traders face the trials of trading and immediately go into a frenzy of making calls on the stock, which is a misinformed reaction. This leaves them vulnerable to losing their heads and money with every change in the financial markets. To avoid this mess, investors should pay attention to what is in their baskets and the relevant information on each dividend stock. This means doing extensive research and knowing the track records of each of the firms that you hold a share in. Having this information at hand will have an investor looking for lucrative deals instead of exiting strategies when the market is hit hard by the changing economic times.

Misinformed Purchase of Stock

A few investors and traders buy stock hastily because of a tip that was given to them. It could have been by a trusted associate or a professional acquaintance or maybe by just listening to the business shows that are all over the television and radio. The ideology that this was a tip given to them by a trusted confidant or a professional in their filed has most traders bypassing the first step of conducting their own investigation into the company's fundamentals. This move proves to be hurtful to their portfolios resulting in losses.

Misinformed Decisions

Novice traders expect to buy the stock a few days before the dividend payment and sell it a couple of days after the payout. This seems like an attractive idea for the trader who will believe they have discovered the best trading strategy. What they fail to account for is the effect of the dividend payout on the prices of the stock. Stock prices will reflect the price of the dividends, and this will result in a breakeven position for the trader who opts to sell their stock after receiving the dividend payment.

Paying Attention to the Returns

Investors who gauge the performance of their investments by looking at the yields often end up in the dividend trap with a string of losses in their portfolios. Failing to understand how a company can have high returns, but the low growth rate is the downfall of most traders and investors. Chasing the paycheck is not the best strategy in dividend investments. It is the best recipe for disaster, though. It results in a mental breakdown and financial draining of the few coins in the bank of the investor, plunging them deeper into the abyss and making them more likely to make even more damaging financial decisions. Investors should have the returns figures at the back of their minds as well as the nitty-gritty details that the stock comes with as a package. If these details are considered risky, it is advisable for the investor to avoid putting a cent into the stock.

Paying Attention to the Present Situation More Than the Future Expectations of the Dividends

The information that is offered is information that is up to date. It mirrors the outcome of the year and the expected price of what the investors will receive in the current financial year. Investors should be interested in the price that the company will pay their dividend stockholders in the next years, maybe five or ten years down the line. The future is very hard to determine, but with the help of a few questions, an investor can have a blurry picture of how it will look like in the near future.

Investors and traders need to be vigilant and pay attention to the:

1. Projections for income that the management has come up with
2. The trend of the company in how they treat their dividend stockholders that is if they prioritize them or neglect them
3. Change that is likely to have an impact on the company's history of having ready cash flow

Monitoring and Evaluation of the Stock

Dividend stock investing does not require constant evaluation like day trading, but it also does not mean that the investor should not pay attention once the purchase is made. Keeping an ear on the ground is important for the investor because the investor will get information first hand, and with the right tapping into the grapevine, they may end up with the information long before it hits the public. There are two advantages to this; the first is as an investor, you get the chance to buy into the stock before the public knows about a major investment decision that will most likely raise the dividend pay off. The second advantage is if the firm is in trouble, as the investor, you are aware of this beforehand, which will give you time to make the necessary adjustments so that your investment portfolio does not take such a hit.

Gambling instead of Investing

The difference between gambling and investing is one involves speculating while the other involves making informed decisions on a future prospect. Investors who gamble with stock buy a stock simply because the price is low regardless of the amount of money that the yield gives. Gamblers do not have a plan to follow or an investment model to work with, they pick what they feel is best and wait for the yields which rarely materialize. To avoid gambling, investors need to stick to the rules and research while avoiding the shortcuts to riches. However, should you do research and spot a good bargain on a company that has a proven track record take the gamble.

Taxation

One of the saddest things about earning high figures is losing a large chunk of that figure to the taxation authorities. The majority of the traders do not take this into consideration and build their reinvestment plans around the full amount they expect to earn. Whenever the taxation cuts happen, they are thrown off the path and into a frenzy. This often materializes into making hasty and rushed decisions in a bid to cover the amount that was taxed, which means they go out of the books and end up recording losses. Keep in mind how much money you make is not as important as what is retained in the account after all the legal processes are done.

These are just examples of the mistakes that most traders make both the seasoned traders and the young novices. There are a lot more mistakes that traders can make in the practice of dividend investing and a lot of hidden holes that one can fall in along the journey. Being aware that the waters can be very rough is the first step any investor can make to avoid the hazardous dangers. We hope that these issues laid bare in this chapter will give the investor an idea of what to be on the lookout for and how to avoid falling into the trap. The second step is reaching out to a professional for help in the navigation of murky dividend investment waters. As the journey progresses, as an investor, you will encounter more issues that will leave you wiser for the next crucial decision that needs to be made and with a keener eye for seeing potential dangers before walking into them. For now, though, we hope this chapter has equipped you better to identify some issues on your own and avoid them.

To help you avoid these mistakes, we stress the importance of discipline and self-control. Traders and investors should exercise patience in their dealings and not rush to jump ship. The trading psychology of the human mind has been analyzed over the years by different experts who came to the conclusion that emotions should not be part of any decision made in trading or investing, whether it is in stock or options or Forex. The desire for the human mind to be rich in a quick way also plays a huge role in these mistakes by investors. We end up thinking and counting our eggs before they hatch, which often leaves us gnawing and gnashing our teeth whenever the hasty moves backfire in our faces.

Chapter 14: How to Succeed While Investing in Dividend Stocks

How to Succeed while Investing in Dividend Stocks

Investing in dividends can be a strategic and intellectual form of acquiring constant income. It is, however, considered a risky business and may result in losses. Being successful while undertaking this type of investment is not hard, but it does require knowledge on the workings of the principles revolving it. There are several things investors can focus on in pursuit of successful investing:

Quality over Quantity

The dividend yield is a significant component used by investors when they want to know which investments they should make. Normally, investors usually have better returns when the yields are high.

Sometimes, the numbers relating to the yields tend to be misleading. It is possible for dividends not to yield anything when the payout levels of a stock cannot be sustained for a long period. Fluctuations are not rare events, and they affect the yields of the dividends.

It is advisable for investors to pick stable investments. They do not involve a lot of risks and are reliable. High-risk investments have higher yields, but they tend to be unreliable during the long run. Stable investments may result in lower yields in the short run, but they are reliable in the long run. Investors who use the buy-and-hold method are more likely to pick stable investments when deciding where to invest.

Established Companies

The stock market can be seen as cyclic. It has the habit of repeating trends every now and then. One of the best ways of deciding investments is by observing the previous performances of the market to know the trend that might repeat itself. Investors should specifically focus on the "aristocrat" companies. These are companies that are already established in the stock market. They have consistently raised their payouts for the past twenty-five years. These are the type of companies investors should look for because they have a steady flow of income, and chances are they will still have steady flows in the future.

Potential for Growth

New companies can sometimes have higher dividend yields than other companies. It is, however, not wise for investors to invest in every new company simply because of the current profits. Investors have to pay attention to the future returns that the company is likely to deliver. They should not only focus on the present profits, but also on the potential for the company to grow and increase their returns. It will be a shame if an investor invests in a new company that currently has a lot of returns but has no potential to increase these returns, or even maintain the returns it currently has.

Value and growth investing are differentiated through this. Growth investing does not look at your current numbers. It focuses on the long-term approach and growth and considers how beneficial it will be for the investor in terms of dividends.

Payout Ratio

A dividend payout ratio is a ratio that shows the amount the stakeholders receive and the amount the company keeps. It is quite important in deciding an investment.

There are companies that have dividend stocks with high yields, but they give their investors in substantial percentages of the yields. Investors should be cautious about such types of companies. These companies can reduce the number of dividends investors receive to non-existent, the moment they feel like their stream of income decreases.

Mix It Up

It is common practice for companies to focus on specifics sectors of a stock market or some specific stocks. They do this to increase their chances of acquiring more dividends and income. Most companies that focus on such things have a good track record, and their success rates are high. However, in the face of a market downtown of shifts in trends, these companies may experience several problems.

To decrease the risk of having all your dividends lost in the case of market downtown, spread out your assets. Diversify the holdings you have by having several investments in different areas. If one of the places you have your dividends suffers a loss, then the rest of your profits are still intact in other areas.

Knowing When to Stay and When to Leave

Warren Buffet, an investment expert, encourages investors to have a long-term view when it comes to investing. He also tells investors to be smart and cut their losses on time. Investors should know when to be patient for the payoff and when to cut their losses and to avoid waiting for too long. Whenever investors buy stocks, they should know if the stock will bring profit in the long or short run. They should always be aware of whether the company will deliver it payoff or whether it will fail. It is a crucial skill to know when to wait out stock and when to back off while you still can.

Keep Your Mind Straight

It is important to have objectives, which are both realistic and attainable. It would be juvenile to simply dive in and search for the stocks with the highest yields. Having common sense and being reasonable should be the mindset an investor has as he embarks in choosing an investment. Using this logic, we cannot have high yields without expecting high risks.

Likewise, we cannot say that we find new trading gems that other investors have not already found. With the increasing popularity of dividend investing, all stocks are examined and cross-examined by trading experts. Before diving into an investment, confirm the facts, as well as the forecasts.

Understanding Dividend Yields and Policies

Dividend policies set up by companies in accordance with the company's objectives and the characteristics of the industry it is in. Investors are drawn to dividends that are stable with high chances of increasing in the long run. Management in these companies knows this. They structure their policies in a way that they pay out less during the profitable times, to be able to retain the dividend during periods with low profits.

It is not uncommon to find companies that are similar to having different dividend yields. The difference can be attributed to different characteristics by the companies. A company may believe that reinvesting earnings is a good way to grow a business. Therefore, it will not pay the investor anything, or it will pay a small amount. By doing this, it will have more prospects in terms of growth. Another company will offer to pay out a good amount of earning. It will attract dividend investors who are interested in quick profits and do not focus on long term growth capabilities.

Stick to Established Companies

The want for even higher dividend yields has led investors into unchartered territory. They move away from the known investment companies and put their focus on areas where the rewards are as high as the risks. These areas are seen to have the desired profits, but they also have hidden risks that cannot be seen by the investors.

The examples of such high profit, high-risk areas include leveraged funds, convertibles, private placements, trusts, and limited partnerships. These areas require a special understanding of "sophisticated" strategies, analysis, and understanding.

It is not always wise to venture into unknown areas of

investments, despite the high risks that may be involved. Investing in these areas may result in losing all the profits you might have acquired. Though buying stocks from already established companies may not be as lucrative in the short term, it ensures you have a steady source of income in the long run.

Financial ratios

In layman's terms, financial ratios are the dividend of the number of investors use to have a better understanding of the opportunities relating to an investment. These ratios can be sourced from different files and documents of the company, such as investor presentations and annual reports. Some of the top financial ratios include:

Dividend Payout Ratio

The most commonly used financial ratio is the dividend payout ratio. It is a measurement of the amount paid as dividends from the earnings of the company.

The calculations for the payout ratio of a company are easy: divide the dividends the company pays over a period by the earnings it has generated.

The dividend payout ratio is helpful to investors because they give more information on the safety of the dividend of the company. It also gives information on future growth possibilities.

High payout ratios are considered to be above 70%. They imply that a lot of the earnings of the company are consumed by the dividend payments, which makes this investment risky. Should a trend fall, the company may not have the profits to pay dividends to the investors. High payout ratios also restrict dividend growth.

The optimum dividend payout ratios range below 60%. Any company with a high payout ratio will only be considered if it is extremely stable. It will also be considered if its health is financially strong.

Free Cash Flow

Free cash flow is necessary for the long-term survival of a company.

The calculation for the free cash flow is the subtraction of the capital expenditure of a company from the operation's cash flow. The capital expenditures are the money used on pieces of equipment or properties, among others. The operations are the adjusted net income for charges like depreciation that do not involve cash.

Free cash flow is essential because its generation ensures a company has the funds to give the shareholders' dividends. It also makes sure that the company has enough cash flow for repaying debts and acquisition.

Investors prefer to have their investments in companies that are able to maintain their free cash flow in whatever environment.

Return on Invested Capital

It is acquiring funds from investors and investing the funds in providing a return. For example, you want to invest $100. One company offers to turn your money into $105, and another into $110. If all other factors are constant, the second company would be the best option because of its faster generation of returns.

Higher returns in companies result in faster compounding of capital. Companies with these traits are usually highly desirable. Companies should be able to earn more returns than the demands of the investors, or else they will go out of business.

When analyzing the return on invested capital of a company, we focus on the consistency and level of the returns. Companies that are efficient and profitable have a stable return on invested capital for several years.

Another financial ratio that is similar to the return in invested capital is the return on equity. Warren Buffet, a renowned investment expert, highly advocates for this ratio. This ratio is the division of the net income of a company by the equity of the shareholders.

Buffet believes that companies have a competitive advantage when they have a higher return on equity. These companies tend to compound earnings quicker than other companies.

One of the main differences between return on equity and return on invested capital is the measurement of debt and equity in the returns of the company by the return on invested capital. This provides for better comparison between companies. It would be more profitable to invest in a company that has fewer returns but no debt, than a company with higher returns and debts.

Operating Profit Margin

It is the division of the operating profits by the total number of sales. It is a representation of the earnings of the company prior to taxes and interests.

When we exclude the expenses, we focus on the operations' profitability brought about by the comparison of the companies. The tax treatments and financials choices are not considered. A signal for having economic moat has higher profit margins.

Similar to the return on invested capital, we tend to focus on the consistency and level of the operating margin of a company. Margins that are stable and high assist in the faster compounding of earnings.

Asset Turnover

The calculation for an asset turnover is the division of the total sales of a company by the assets.

High asset turnover allows companies to have good returns in the invested capital, despite having low margins. These companies can get more profits since their assets generated plenty of sales. The companies effectively use their assets to their benefit. An excellent example of such a company is Wal-Mart. It has a low-profit margin but generates a double-digit return since it has a high asset turnover.

Sales Growth

It is the subtraction of the revenue of one period from the revenue of another period. It is expressed as the percentage of the first revenue.

Sales growth gives us more information on the ability of a company to continuously expand, and the company's business model's volatility.

Companies that have cyclic growths should not be considered when they are at peak demand, because it is a sure way to lose money.

Net Debt-To-Capital

This ratio shows the amount of debt used to run a company. Debts are cumbersome burdens, whether they are mortgages or debts from credit cards. Borrowing money to cater to our wants and needs is a dangerous game, including in companies.

The ratio explains the finance portion of the company that was acquired through debt. Its calculation is the division of the total book debt by itself, plus equity.

Investors should not invest in companies that have more than

50% debt to capital ratio. Companies that may have a lot of debt may be unable to pay the debt. It may lead to the crushing of their stock prices and low or non-existent dividend payments.

Net Debt

This ratio is a focus of the debt of a company to its earnings. The concept around this ratio is companies that generate high profits are less risky despite having a lot of debt. Net debt is calculated by the subtraction of the cash a company has at hand from the total debt.

Price-To-Earnings Ratio

It is a commonly used metric. It is the division of the stock price by the earnings a share a company generates yearly. Throughout history, the P/E multiple has ranged around 15 for the market. Earnings by companies are considered stable when their earnings multiples are higher than the markets. P/E ratios of 20 or less are optimum when it comes to choosing companies to invest in.

Total Shareholder Return

There exists an urge, by dividend investors, to look at the yields alone, since they are the profitable returns. Investors, however, should still focus on total returns. There would be no benefit in yielding a 6% dividend, but the price of the stock decreases by nearly half.

Total shareholder return is the measurement of the increment of the price of a stock, together with any dividends. Its calculation is the addition of the increased stock price and the dividend per share, divided by the subtraction of one from the previous stock price.

Over time, businesses that are well-managed are obliged to manage shareholder value. They do this by delivering a return, which lines up with the market, at the very least.

Analysis by financial ratios is only valuable if there are significant insights that come with them. When using financial ratios in dividend investing, we focus on the identification of steady profits and dividend that grows with time. It is, therefore, important to understand the financial ratios you may use when choosing your investments. The ratios may not always be effective, but they will help you avoid numerous mistakes that come with investing. They increase your chances of being successful in dividend investing.

Research and Independent Thinking

Investing as a practice is full of randomness and uncertainty. It is important for an investor to think for himself and decide on the best investments he should make.

In this day and age, blindly, the following advice from online sources or so-called internet investment experts may not result in the profits you hope for. The advice they give work for them, but you are not assured of their strategies working for you.

Therefore, it is important to carry out your own research. There are plenty of materials available for sufficient research on different stocks and companies. Carrying out this researches will give you a better chance of knowing what will benefit you in the short and long run. Research goes hand in hand with being able to make your own decisions. By having substantial knowledge of your investment choices, you can choose the right companies to invest in that will result in higher dividends, and work towards your goals.

Acquiring Financial Literacy

You do not need an investment expert to invest in stocks, but you do need to be informed about the working of the trade, the interpretation of financial statements, and accounting in general.

Through a thorough understanding of financial concepts is significant; you do not need to analyze and look at hundreds of financial statements relating to companies and investments. You can get financial data from the internet, which allows you to remain informed in simple steps. There are also investment tools that show the data needed about a company. These tools and data give you the literacy required to make informed decisions on the dividend investments you want to make.

Remain Informed and Do Not over Manage Their Portfolios

It is not uncommon, especially for new investors, to watch their investment portfolios all the time, like hawks. They are worried about the losses, gains, and risks that come with investing. A lot of companies also overanalyze the slight changes in the prices of their stocks. They emphasize the events that occur during the short-term, despite these events having little influence on their values and stock. New investors tend to follow the footsteps of such companies and also over manage their own investments.

Managing dividend portfolios requires patience and focus on

long-term goals. Constantly worrying about the stocks that may appreciate or depreciate every day will not always benefit investors. They should aim at having quality companies, and allow these companies to grow their dividends and compound in value.

We need to keep in mind that underlying business fundamentals are less volatile than stock prices. This knowledge will help us understand that we should focus on the long-term goal and not worry about short-term occurrences. Instead of micro-managing portfolios, dividend investors should monitor developments every now and then, choosing their stock with the mindset of a long-term holding and profit.

Dividend investments are lucrative when undertaken using the rightful approach. To be successful in dividend investment, investors should have the necessary information, mindset, and the ability to know which investment will give high profits while reducing risks.

Conclusion

With the content provided in the book, I believe that you are now in a position of investing in dividend stocks. I cannot say that I have fully exhausted all the information that one needs to learn, however, that which is present can act as a good startup. As an individual, it is important that you are always ready and willing to learn. There is plenty of knowledge and information to be acquired. With the right attitude to learn, there is a lot that you can pick from books, people, internet sources, and other learning materials. It is without any doubt that dividend stocks are a worthwhile investment. There are some individuals that have created wealth out of investing in dividend stocks. Anyone can do this, and it is not only limited to specific people. The secret to making it in any industry is having mastery of how it operates. Once you have identified the loopholes and acquired a few successful tactics and strategies, then you are good to go. One also has to be willing to put more effort into what they do to ensure that they get better each day. Learning more about your investment allows you do discover new things each time. Such discoveries influence your productivity in that given field. As you decide to engage in dividend stocks, be open to learning and researching. This allows you to make the right decisions that you will not regret later on. Take your time learning and making new discoveries.

As you decide to invest in dividend stocks, it is also important that you get a mentor. The mentor can be one that is already in the industry and flourishing in it, and such a person can offer good guidance that will be beneficial while investing. While at it, training can be effective in ensuring that you acquire the information necessary to succeed in the industry. Most times, we make quick decisions that lead us in the wrong direction. The information allows us to avoid such instances, and therefore, we make the right choices that impact us in a positive way. With the information provided, any beginner can comfortably learn how to invest in a dividend stock. The same applies to individuals who are already in the industry. They can learn of the best measures to make that can guarantee their future in the investment industry. In case you were previously stuck or some things remained unclear, now you have acquired some information. From this point, learning never stops. Ensure that you keep finding more materials that you can use in your learning process and get to know more regarding investing in dividend stocks. The first step of making a decision sets everything ablaze and allows things to move as anticipated. In case you have been thinking of investing in dividend stocks, now is the best time to do so. All you need to do is make the decision and jump straight into it. You are at least assured of an interesting journey now that you have some tips on how to go about it.

CPSIA information can be obtained
at www.ICGtesting.com
Printed in the USA
LVHW022301131120
671604LV00008B/241